# How to Bake a Book

### A textbook on creative writing

## Nod Ghosh

*How to Bake a Book* copyright © Nod Ghosh
First published as a book May 2025 by Everytime Press

ISBN: 978-1-923000-82-7

Also available as an eBook
ePub ISBN: 978-1-923000-86-5
Kindle ISBN: 978-1-923000-90-2

BP#00136

All rights reserved by the author and publisher.
Except for brief excerpts used for review or scholarly purposes,
no part of this book may be reproduced in any manner whatsoever
without express written consent of the publisher or the author.

Everytime Press
32 Meredith Street
Sefton Park  SA  5083
Australia

Email: everytimepress@outlook.com
Website: https://everytimepress.com/
Everytime Press catalogue:
https://everytimepress.com/everytime-press-catalogue/

Front cover original idea copyright © Matt Potter
Front cover original spoon design copyright © Nod Ghosh
Front cover original spoon photograph (portion) copyright © leopictures

Everytime Press is a member of the
**Bequem Publishing collective**
bequempublishing.com

To Eileen Merriman,

who understands the essence
of a good book.

# Contents

| | | |
|---|---|---|
| 1 | Prologue | |
| | *A Blind Salesman Moment* | |
| 9 | Chapter One | |
| | *The (Almost) Infinite Freezer* | |
| 20 | Chapter Two | |
| | *I Don't Go to Nursery – The Art of Active Reading* | |
| 29 | Chapter Three | |
| | *Word Choices* | |
| 39 | Chapter Four | |
| | *Different Genres* | |
| 51 | Chapter Five | |
| | *Story Structure* | |
| 63 | Chapter Six: | |
| | *Sets & Drugs & Rock & Roll & Shady Characters* | |
| 76 | Chapter Seven | |
| | *Respect, and a Question* | |
| 87 | Chapter Eight | |
| | *The Answer to the Question* | |
| 89 | Chapter Nine | |
| | *Getting Your Work Out There* | |
| 101 | Chapter Ten | |
| | *Writers' Block and What's-the-Pointism* | |

| | |
|---|---|
| 107 | Chapter Eleven<br>*The Writing Community* |
| 120 | Chapter Twelve<br>*Other Ingredients for a Book* |
| 129 | Chapter Thirteen<br>*Ancillary Activities* |
| 135 | Chapter Fourteen<br>*Where to Next?* |
| 145 | Extra Exercises |
| 165 | List of Recipes |
| 167 | List of Exercises |
| 169 | Author Acknowledgements |
| 171 | About the Author |

# Prologue

## A Blind Salesman Moment

They arrived at 8.17 a.m.

I'd been expecting them at 8.30 a.m.

They were coming to clean my windows. Daylight savings had ended the previous night. Everyone was up early – including me. I'd been clearing clutter from windowsills and moving furniture.

At 8.10 a.m., twenty minutes before they were due, I thought, "Shit. I'd better hop into the shower. Don't want to be wandering about in my dressing gown when they arrive." And I wasn't.

In a dressing gown, I mean, when they knocked on the door.

I only had time to grab a tiny towel and wrap it around myself.

I let the two young men in. My hair dripped on the carpet. Perhaps my bum was showing, I'll never know. I didn't ask. They were courteous and business-like. The three of us acted as if there was nothing untoward about a half-naked geriatric opening the door to strangers at 8.17 in the morning.

They're doing a great job as I write. They've opted to start working on the outside.

How does this relate to baking a book?

It doesn't.

It's included to show life is chaotic.

No matter how well you timetable, other factors influence events.

Always expect the unexpected.

This is a book about creative writing.

It might not be what you expect.

The book will hopefully be useful for people who are embarking on the "journey", as well as those with more experience.

*How to Bake a Book* contains exercises that should work for most people.

There are recipes in here too because completing a piece of writing, whether it is micro-fiction or a series of novels, is a form of alchemy, like baking a cake.

Here's the first recipe:

## Chocolate Almond Cake

This cake never fails to please, unless you know people who don't like chocolate. But those people are hard to please anyway. The cake is wheat free, which is useful for people who can't / don't eat wheat. I copied it from an operating manual named "recipes" in the laboratory where I work.

No one knows where it came from.

## Ingredients

- 200g chopped dark chocolate (e.g. 70% cocoa butter)
- 150g butter, chopped
- 5 eggs, separated
- ¾ cup = 190mL caster sugar
- 1½ cups almond meal

## Method

- Pre-heat oven to 160°C.
- Grease / line a 22 cm diameter cake tin.
- Melt butter and chocolate together. (Up to four x thirty-second bursts in microwave oven, depending on power. Stir the mixture after each burst to check.)
- Set aside chocolate mix to cool until finger hot, and then stir in egg yolks, sugar and almonds.
- In a separate bowl, whisk egg whites until stiff peaks form.
- Fold the egg whites into the choc mix until just combined.
- Spoon mixture into the prepared cake tin.
- Bake for 55 minutes (check at 45 minutes) until an inserted skewer comes out dry.
- Cool completely in tin.
- Dust with icing sugar.
- Or top with a ganache.

## Ganache

- Melt 200g dark chocolate with ½ to ¾ cup of cream (thirty second bursts as above).
- Mix and allow to cool.
- Pour over cake.
- Chill.

I like the final step, though it's not an easy instruction to follow in more ways than one.

Here's the first exercise:

# Ten Minutes When You Must Write

You want to write, but you're too busy to start. If that's you, do this exercise now. If you won't do it now, set your alarm ten minutes early tomorrow morning and do it then.

## Ingredients

- something to write with
- something to time ten minutes with

## Method

- Preparation required: none
- Write for ten minutes without stopping

It doesn't matter what you write about.
It doesn't matter if you don't feel inspired.
It doesn't matter if you haven't had the "big idea" yet.
It doesn't matter if what you write is bollocks.

Have ten minutes passed yet?
↓
No
↓
Keep going

Have ten minutes passed yet?

Yes

Stop

Look over what you've written. You may have the bones of a story, or there may not appear to be anything salvageable. Save it anyway. Save everything. Never throw out cake scraps or trimmings. They can be used for making trifles, or cake-filled moulded chocolate shapes.

Create a folder for your writing "stubs".

Save those middle-of-the-night brilliant ideas in a folder too.

Freeze your cake scraps in sandwich bags or airtight containers.

If you don't sleep with your phone near you, keep a note pad and pen at your bedside for those wondrous ideas that wake you up at 3.17 a.m. When you read them the next morning, you'll discover ninety-nine per cent of those Booker Prize-esque flurries are horse faeces. One per cent might have the potential to be developed into a reasonable poem or short story – or a Booker Prize-winning novel.

No. Forget that last one. I was only kidding.

All the same, never throw anything away. Horse faeces has its uses. Sometimes you need fertiliser to nourish your ideas.

Where does the blind salesman come into it?

This is an oblique reference to the old question, "Whom are you writing for?"

Do you want to sell your product? Is your writing marketable? Are you willing to knock from door to proverbial door to get your work out there? How far will you compromise your art in order to please your customer? Are you blinded by rumours about current publishing trends?

You may have encountered behavioural analysis strategies, for example, workplace-profiling systems used by prospective employers. There's one that's questionnaire based, which places applicants into quadrants of a pie chart according to their strengths: dominatrix, influencer, constipated or submissive. (I can't exactly remember the categories so I may be misquoting.) When the applicant is told their result they are informed no outcome is better or worse than any other.

There is no right answer.

"Whom are you writing for?" is the same.

There's no *right answer*.

But will people like your writing? Will it sell? If so, who will distribute your work?

When it comes to marketing, there are times in your writing career when it's a *good* thing your work isn't published, read or remunerated. Take most pre-teen angst-ridden poetry that can be found in shoeboxes in attics all over the world. Believe me, it's good if most of that stuff stays there.

There will be other times when "getting your work out" matters. There's more about this in "Getting Your Work Out There" (chapter nine), but success might be a by-product of striving for entirely different goals, motivated by something other than wanting to be published. So whom *are* you writing for?

There is no right answer.

Don't let people stamp on your dreams. It's all right to dream. But if you want to keep those dreams safe, be careful whom you tell them to. Look at it from the other perspective. It's not uncommon for people who *have a book in them* (or two or three) to broadcast the fact that they are going to publish said Booker Prize winner, describe which authors they'll emulate, what their cover designs will be and who will play the protagonist in the film version … if and when they finally get around to writing the thing. You don't want to be that person.

Like most skills, it takes practice to hone the craft of writing.

This isn't a universal truth. Some pre-teen angst-ridden poetry is actually good, just as some pre-school painters produce art that is composed well and nuanced with subtle undertones. But those young poets probably haven't written because they didn't fancy the options the school careers advisor suggested and instead decided to make a living from writing. They likely wrote because they *had to.*


That's not to say you should never write for a target.

You might enter writing competitions. It's wise to read and understand the remit.

You may look up previously successful entries to gauge the aesthetic or tone. But don't copy the judge's writing style hoping it will appeal, because they'll likely see straight through you as easily as my newly-cleaned windows. Likewise, when submitting to journals, familiarise yourself with their content.

Unless your piece can be redrafted to suit the publication, it's best to save it for somewhere else.

So why have I mentioned submitting to journals when the title of this book is *How to Bake a **Book***? There are multitudes of online and print journals that publish poetry, flash fiction, short stories and creative non-fiction. Submitting to these publications is a good way to hone your skills. Some even offer feedback. I'll elaborate on this in "Getting Your Work Out There" (chapter nine).

Full length books such as novels are different, but more on that later.

Eventually, you might use previously published pieces in a single author collection. (You'll need to know whether the original publisher retains rights, and for how long.)

Being broadly published on a smaller scale is a good way of getting yourself known. It can lead to opportunities. It also allows you to connect with other writers.

This introduction has jumped the gun a bit in terms of discussing the business of making a book and how to sell it.

First you have to learn to write.

One of the best ways to do this is to enrol in a writing course. Sorry, although this book will cover some elements a course may provide, it cannot replace the one-to-one feedback offered by an experienced tutor or mentor. It cannot provide the camaraderie of fretting, arguing and critiquing with classmates. Neither can it provide the joy experienced when someone bakes a cake and bring it to share.

What it can do, hopefully, is surprise and enlighten you.

Be prepared for the unexpected.

# Chapter One

## The (Almost) Infinite Freezer

Never throw anything away.

This morning, I was looking for lost things I knew I hadn't discarded. One was a submission to a journal I'd made so long ago, I couldn't remember where I'd filed the work. The editor wanted a contributor agreement, but hadn't included the name of the piece in their correspondence. I needed to locate the story.

We'd also run out of bread. I knew there was half a loaf in the freezer, but it had buried itself amongst leftovers, undesirable frozen vegetables and unidentifiable items that have probably been there since the turn of the century.

Finally, I wanted a fresh idea for a new piece of writing because the deadline for a competition was looming. (It's tomorrow.) I had a character X in mind who'd appeared in other stories, but I wanted to put them in a new situation. I needed to re-read the earlier pieces, because it's faster than developing a character from scratch when working to time constraints. I also wanted "triggers" that would act as prompts to accelerate the plot and make it less predictable.

This is what I found:

Frozen spinach (lots)
When the sky runs a fever, it takes a special god to slow the sun's transit.

temPtation is an unoccuPied ciTy

She cuts legs with the strength of a hero.

## Smacking isn't a language

Ice cubes

Doll-pootool er moton shajiay boshaychhillo, noton bor khojbar jono
they dressed her as a doll for her debut into the marriage market

**He'd fart like a trombone after eating onions.**

It's the idea of being dead while I'm alive I find unpalatable.
Cake scraps frozen in sandwich bags and airtight containers.

her hair is custard blond

~~gluten free moist apple cake~~

cnf in a messenger post

I am chimera. I am diaspora. I am disease.

I am waste. I am wanton destruction.

Under the umlaut

It was more the unbearable happiness of it.

## Half a loaf of brown bread. Hooray!

My submission from over a year ago. Double hooray!

All the stories character X had previously appeared in, and a load of "snippets" to send them into orbit. Triple hooray!

It helped that I have a system for my writing. (Sadly, I can't say the same for the freezer). Most writers probably use electronic means to store work, rather than using paper copies. Either way, a robust filing system is helpful.

Create folders that house all categories of your writing. These may expand as you become more established. They might include:

Separate folders containing different types of writing, e.g. poetry, flash fiction, short stories, plays, scripts, non-fiction and novels.

Make folders for each story containing numbered, dated copies for each redraft.

Adopt codes so you know when something is out on submission, e.g.: a prefix letter to move them to one place in the list. Add the name of the publication as a suffix. Remove both after a rejection, so it's clear the piece is available for recycling. Move published work into a separate folder retaining the suffix (name of the publication – this is important if you need to check whether rights have reverted to you, when re-publishing, as mentioned in the prologue).

It is useful to compile annual submission spreadsheets recording correspondence from publications, their contact details and whether the work has been accepted or rejected. Clearly annotate simultaneous submissions. (I add comments in red.)

Create a separate folder for other people's work that you critique.

File your bios and cover letters in a logical manner. There's more on biographies in "Getting Your Work Out There" (chapter nine).

Save interviews you've given or articles you've written, as you may need them for author questionnaires.

Make a note of "services to the industry", e.g. competition judging, anthology editing.

Keep notes from workshops, festivals and courses attended.

Save technical information, such as notes on grammar or structure.

Keep legal documents such as publishing agreements, preferably backed up electronically in addition to hard copies.

Collect recommendations for marketing strategies.

Have a folder for business accounts. Complete details as soon as you make or receive a payment, so tax returns are less arduous.

Create a blank template document you can copy for new work, using your preferred font, line spacing, page numbering, footer information, etc.

Give some thought to backing your work up. This might be on the cloud, on separate hardware, hard copies or in a "back-ups" email folder. Back "works-in-progress" up regularly.

It's useful to keep two writing CVs. One only you will ever see, which contains everything you've published, and every imaginable source of experience. Add forthcoming publications at the end, and move into the "published" area when released. Then compile a "sanitised" version, containing highlights only, which is ready to send out at short notice if publishers need them.

You may wish to create a website. Good housekeeping is important there too. Regularly check whether any links are still active.

A social media presence is useful for promotion.

This might be a good place to mention courtesy. I'm not saying every literary publisher behaves in a courteous manner, but *you* need to. Bear in mind, many journals rely on the goodwill of unpaid readers and editors. Plus many people know a lot of other people in the field. Be careful. You might be hacked off with someone because of an oversight, but that same person may help you in a different situation in future. It's funny hearing stories about contributors who write back ranting about the rejection of their potential Pulitzer winner. You don't want to be that person.

I'm glad I found the bread. We had avocado toast for lunch.

As for that new piece of writing featuring character X, it's still eluding me. But that's because I've been writing this chapter. The apparently random snippets tucked between the spinach and bread above came from my "stubs" folder. Many were excerpts edited from stories because they were superfluous. Others were part complete pieces. Some came from saved URLs for news articles that triggered the imagination. There were overheard sentences I'd recorded on scraps of paper in cafés, shops and the laboratory where I work.

As a side issue, I hope conversations writers have heard *me* having may have provided source material. When my daughter was four, we were walking to the toyshop so she could spend her birthday money. She knew exactly what she wanted.

"What's the first thing you'd like to look at with your magnifying glass?" I asked, as we crossed the road.

"Diarrhoea," she replied with absolute confidence.

A woman walking in the other direction nearly collapsed with laughter.

I hope she was a writer, and put that to good use.

Sorry for the distraction.

Some of the snippets in the list above were elusive ideas that woke me at 3.17 in the morning.

None of the above were needed at the time, so I'd put them away for later. Therein lies a powerful tool. If you've heard the expression "kill your darlings", you will be painfully aware of how it sometimes takes someone else to point out a treasured aspect of your writing has to go. It could be a character, an overused word, an obsolete storyline, flash back / forward where linear would work as well. They are your darlings because you have worked hard to create them, or you may have other reasons for an emotional attachment.

But someone else can see a problem.

You don't have to follow their advice. However, try changing the "darling" or taking it out. You might write several alternatives. Be honest. Don't do this exercise assuming you can't improve the original, otherwise you'll subliminally sabotage the substitutes.

Have you made a genuine improvement?

You know what to do next.

But put the discarded work in your "stubs" folder and it won't seem so much like bereavement.


Here's a (sort of) recipe:

## Cake-filled Moulded Chocolate Shapes

This isn't a recipe as such, but a suggested activity.

A bunch of YouTube videos appeared in the early 2020s with instructions to make moulded chocolate treats using flexible silicone moulds. Geometric heart shapes were quite popular, for some reason. I sourced a tray of six of them online, each cavity about 6cm in diameter, and 4cm deep. They look like six heads belonging to Kryten from the television series "Red Dwarf", but in pink silicone, and inverted.

## Ingredients & Method

- You'll need leftover cake scraps. The YouTube clips suggest binding cake crumbs with regular buttercream, but we always have little tubs of leftover cream cheese icing in our freezer, from when we make carrot cakes. The tiny amounts are ideal, because you don't need a lot. Cream cheese frosting elevates these treats to gourmet level.
- Wipe out the moulds with vodka or rum before adding chocolate, as this gives a high gloss finish. Some videos suggest tempering real chocolate. Although this would no doubt taste better and have a satisfying "snapping" texture, tempering is a long-winded process involving a candy-thermometer that's guaranteed to make me lose my temper. It's easier to use compound chocolate or candy melts.
- I melt the chocolate in incremental bursts in silicone containers in the microwave oven in the same way as I would when making ganache (see *Chocolate Almond Cake*, page 3).
- If you want to "paint" designs onto the moulds that will appear on the outer surface, use oil-based food colouring to colour white compound chocolate. (Water-soluble colours make the chocolate clump.)
- You need space in your freezer for this, so it's one occasion I've wished for an infinite freezer. I suppose it wouldn't have been a

problem when I lived in student accommodation in the north of England in my youth. You had to scrape ice off the *inside* of the windows in winter. I could have put chocolate on the sill to set. But I wouldn't have been able to afford compound chocolate in those days, or cake ingredients, and silicone moulds hadn't been invented. Neither had Kryten.
- After each chocolate layer is painted or scooped onto the silicone, sit the mould on a hard surface and pop into the freezer while you prepare the next step. You may need two coats for the outer "shell".
- Mush the cake bits and cream cheese icing together and fill the chilled chocolate shells, leaving about 5mm at the top (which will be the bottom).
- Chill again. (I love all this chilling.)
- Cap the cake mix with more chocolate to seal it in.
- After chilling again, push out of moulds and "flatten the bottoms" on a sheet of greaseproof paper on a warm frying pan for a few seconds.
- Chill again, and decorate as desired.
- If you've already painted a design on the outer surface, that might be all you need. If you don't want to invest in oil-based colours, you can "glue" sugar sprinkles on using melted chocolate. If you're flamboyant, do both.

Here's the exercise for this chapter:

## **Recycled Sandwich**

Never throw anything away. This is a way of developing work that isn't quite "there" yet. For example, you may have pieces that have been redrafted and rejected a few times.

### **Ingredients**

- two pieces of writing.

This exercise works well for flash fiction or prose poems. However, you could try chapters from a novel. It's easier to do electronically, but you can do it by hand. You'll need scissors, glue and a lot of patience.

### **Method**

- Note the word count or length of each piece and then hack them roughly in half by editing ruthlessly. (You know what to do with any "darlings".)
- Insert one piece into the middle of the other. Things will be a little messed up. For example, there may be continuity errors. Characters might interact with others whom they haven't yet met. Day might become night and vice versa.
- Edit the piece to make sense of it.

• Could leaving one of the "errors" in add depth or a sense of mystery?

This is an extreme version of seeing a piece of writing from a different perspective when editing. It may be that you revert to your original two pieces. But, you may find something appears as a result of your edit, which can be incorporated into the relevant original piece.

Other ways of seeing work from different perspectives include changing the tense, point of view or even the font, unless you've written longhand.

Try reading the work out loud.

Try reading the words in a different accent.

Put them through Google Translate and convert into a different language. Then translate them back.

Until you think about how these algorithms work, you might expect the results to be the same as the original. They aren't always. Take the two sentences above:

"Put them through Google Translate and convert **to** a different language. Then translate **it again**."

Huh? How did turning them into Swahili and back again do that?

Do any of these exercises prompt you to change the original?

You might find you now have three stories when you started with one.

Never throw anything away.

Hopefully, you can be more ruthless by being less ruthless. I touched upon this briefly in the prologue. If you file rather than discard, you can redraft more boldly.

Enjoy those filled chocolate shapes. Silicone muffin pans work just as well, if you don't want to invest in the Kryten mould.

The bread was the hardest item to retrieve. Maybe I should throw out those dodgy items from my (non-infinite) freezer.

# Chapter Two

## I Don't Go to Nursery – The Art of Active Reading

When our oldest child was small, she had several catch phrases. (This is the kid who liked looking at stuff under high magnification.) Some of her sayings remained in the family vernacular for decades. They serve as examples of how a young human acquires language.

"I don't go to nursery," was one such aphorism. It didn't mean our daughter didn't attend daycare as a preschooler. We both worked full time, so she had to. It was more a command than a statement, a plaintive cry, often worse on a Monday morning, and it very clearly meant, "I don't *want to* go to nursery."

My partner and I still say, "I don't go to nursery," when we don't want to go where we should be going, especially at the start of the week. Not that the laboratory where I work resembles a child care facility, though we have considered installing fold out beds to accommodate an afternoon snooze.

Our second kid spoke a different language. It took weeks for us to decipher "Nomonnit". He would cry, "Nomonnit, nomonnit, nomonnit," as we prepared to leave the house in the mornings.

When we reached the front door, he'd sit on the threshold and remove his trousers. This was a clue, but it had nothing to do with potty training. It actually meant the same as, "I don't go to nursery."

Nomonnit = No want it = I don't want it.

So what's this chapter about? Very little to do with the above, I'm afraid, except in the loosest possible sense.

In our early education, we are encouraged to keep records of what we read. At writing school, our class was encouraged to keep a reading record too.

Actually, I already had a small notebook where I recorded titles of books I'd borrowed. This was so when I grew (even) older, I'd have an aide memoire to remind me what I'd already read. I'm not sure why I thought this was important. If I were to experience the level of dementia that allowed me to forget a title and author, I probably wouldn't remember the story, so the experience would be like reading a fresh book.

Why is reading important if you want to make a book?

You need to read to write. And you need to read analytically.

Imagine trying to invent a cake recipe if you'd never eaten cake. It's not impossible. Someone, somewhere, must have invented the first cake. Remember those occasional angst-ridden teenagers who pull superlative poetry from their nethers without ever studying sonnets, visiting villanelles or poring over pantoums?

I mentioned earlier that it was a good idea to enrol in a writing course if you want to make a book. Reading is as important, if not more so.

After finishing writing school, I wasn't yet a particularly proficient writer. Learning is a lifelong process. (Sorry for the cliché.) I've learned further techniques from critique partners over the years. One person is so adept, she practically inhales a book in the time it takes me to eat a sandwich. I've learned a tremendous amount from this person. What she's absorbed from reading well-chosen books informs her writing, which in turn has helped re-shape mine.

Be selective. Try new forms. Challenge yourself. I turned to historical fiction as I recognised it wasn't something I usually chose. Later I began to write it.

Read critically. How has the writer introduced characters? What about plot? Pacing? Tension? Story arc?

Read carefully, but also read for fun. Read widely. Read in different ways. Skim, picking out keywords to form an overall impression. Scan to find areas you are particularly interested in.

You likely employ different types of reading in different situations.

You read workplace communications in a particular way, which may be different from how you read a news article. Following instructions requires a different skill, for example, when assembling flat pack furniture. This sort of reading can result in *what-the-fuckitis*, for which there is no known cure.

Remember that Google Translate exercise? Translating into a language you don't speak is another sort of alchemy, but the end product isn't as satisfying as cake. I wish the flat pack industry would realise this.

My current "reading record" contains notes on the books I've read, along with an analysis of what I've learned. I might add a brief synopsis (the dementia thing could still happen). If I really like the work, I might polish my notes and submit a review somewhere. I generally don't review books I don't rate highly. I think other people are probably better at writing dastardly scathing reviews than I'd be.

Sometimes family and friends ask whether being an over-analytical dick about books interferes with my enjoyment of literature. It can do. Occasionally, I have to remind myself to *let go* and simply enjoy the thing.

I'm not a good person to watch films with. My mother was worse. If she'd already seen a movie, she'd reveal the ending just before the climax. I have an excuse for being a pain. Films are useful for studying story structure. But sometimes I forget to let my partner enjoy an "aha!" moment when she works out whodunnit. Instead, I offer an analysis of whether the foreshadowing is too obvious, too subtle, or just right.

Hmmm. Whodunnit = Who done it = Who committed the crime?

Perhaps our kid was speaking in crime-mystery-fictionese?

It's probably irritating for normal humans to be told something shows the Rashomon effect or is following a monomyth narrative, when all they want to know is whether the character gets it on with their love interest and if the popcorn is any good.

You know what I'm going to say, don't you? Even though I have been that person, you *don't* want to be that person.

They're an arsehole.

There is another reason I began this chapter with an illustration of how humans acquire language. In many of the arts, you have to learn a great deal about the form, only for much of what you've learned not to show in your work. Bizarre as it sounds, I feel you need a wide vocabulary in order to write in plain clear language.

We model some of our behaviour on what our parents showed us. For other things we find our own way.

I've chosen not to give away the endings of films I have seen before, when watching them with someone else.

Sorry, Mum.

There's one habit I have continued. I call it "mum's the word", even though I learned it from my dad. My father used to write down new words he came across in a notebook. Later, he'd look up a dictionary definition.

I used to be hesitant about using certain words I was familiar with, but not confident about their meaning. I vaguely knew them, but felt embarrassed looking them up, until I began collecting them in notebooks – now electronic folders – with the cagey name. "Mum's the word" implied a covert operation. Investigating a word's origin, discovering its synonyms and antonyms, and looking at examples of its use, elevates it to the realm of the familiar.

Before we leave the theme of habits we've picked up from our early education, this might be a good place to mention timetabling.

Have you had the school nightmare? The bell has rung. You have five minutes to cross the school campus to get to your next class, which might be double biology in the science block, or it might be English in the old building on the other side of the grounds. Or is it maths? And where the fuck is maths? Younger people, bear with me. I know schools aren't like that anymore. But this is my nightmare. Not only do you have no idea what class you're supposed to be going to, or where anything is, but isn't there an exam you need to sit?

Timetables don't have to induce stress. They can be helpful. Ever found that when you've had more time available you've become less productive? That's likely because busy people have neatly constructed timetables. When it's time for double maths / working through a copy edit from a publisher / writing chapter two of *How to Bake a Book,* you are *only* doing that thing, and you damn well make sure you do it, because when the bell goes, you'll not be able to do it any more. I'll touch on this again in "Ancillary Activities" (chapter thirteen). It's one way in which constraints can be helpful. You don't need to take a break to see who's posted a funny meme on social media, because you're going to get a break in a few minutes anyway.

Great idea in theory, but it's bloody hard work tearing yourself away for a walk in the sun when you're tantalisingly close to finishing the next chapter.

Good luck with that.

Here's the recipe for this chapter:

## Gluten-free Moist Apple Cake

Apologies to those who dislike the M-word. I don't know why "moist" gets such bad press, but it's something to consider when we look at word choices later. My personal pet-hates are "gotten" and "atop". I guess it's subjective.

I've tried to emulate a dense cake I sampled at a party once. I never discovered who made it, so I couldn't ask for the recipe. However, after three or four attempts, I arrived at something almost as good.

## Ingredients

- 1½ cups gluten free flour (one cup = 250mL)
- ½ cup almond meal
- ¾ tsp baking soda
- ½ tsp salt
- 1 tsp ground cinnamon
- 1 tsp ground cloves
- 1 tsp ground nutmeg
- 1 tsp ginger powder
- ½ cup brown sugar plus 2 tbsp for topping
- 2 tbsp honey
- 1½ tsp vanilla extract
- 1 cup vegetable oil
- 2 beaten eggs
- 3 apples, peeled, cored and cut into thin slices
- ¾ cup crushed walnuts
- butter for greasing
- optional extra: seasonal ripe fruit e.g. 2 sliced tamarillos, or ½ cup blueberries

## Method

- Preheat oven to 180°C.
- Grease a 21cm square pan with butter.
- Sprinkle 2 tbsp sugar over the butter.
- Lay "optional extras" if used over the butter / sugar layer.
- Place flours, baking soda, salt and spices in a bowl. Whisk to combine.
- In a separate bowl, whisk oil and sugar.
- Add honey, which will initially cause sugar to clump.

- Add eggs and vanilla. Continue whisking, and the sugar should disperse.
- Pour wet ingredients onto dry and mix lightly.
- Stir apple slices and walnuts through mixture, and carefully pour over the prepared pan, without disturbing toppings (if used).
- Bake for 40 minutes (check at 30 minutes) until an inserted skewer comes out dry.
- Cool in the pan.

Here's the exercise for this chapter:

## Emulation

You've always wanted to write like Ernest Hemingway or E.L. James, though you don't want to copy them.

## Ingredients

- a book by a writer you admire
- a different book
- imagination

## Method

- Set a scene by opening the *different book* at random.
- The page number you have selected must be incorporated as a date in your story. For example, p8 could be the 8th of February, or

p347 could be March 1847. The *3* is for March, and *47* the year in the century of choice. It could be the actual date the story is set in, or it may be featured: the character might discover a letter in the attic dated 15th March 1847.

• Close your eyes and point to a word in the different book. Use that word to form the setting your character(s) will find themselves in. Your location might *sound like* the word, or be associated with it. For example, "execute" becomes "Exeter", or "fire" becomes "hell".

• Locate the ISBN of the different book. The last two digits are the age of a character in your piece.

• Write a scene in the style of the writer whose work you admire, *but* you can only glimpse at their book for as long as you can hold your breath. Then you must close it and write at least three sentences before you look at it again. This time too, you're only allowed to look at it for as long as you can hold your breath. Try not to die. Write at least three more sentences before looking at the primary book another time.

• Keep writing in this way for at least fifteen minutes, but no longer than thirty.

How did that go? Did the constraints help or hinder you in emulating the style? Either way, hopefully the exercise has made you think about what the *essence* of your admired writer's work is, albeit at the risk of causing you to suffocate.

Enjoy the moist cake.

# Chapter Three

## Word Choices

The reason I attended writing school wasn't due to my ambition to be an author. There was a series of distinct steps that led me there.

We migrated to New Zealand in the early naughties. I discovered Kiwi English has specific qualities. To demonstrate approval, we say, "Sweet as," without stating *what* something is as sweet as. Apparently, we are the only English speakers who refer to flimsy rubber sandals as "jandals". Our cool boxes are known as "chilly bins". Australians keep their beer cold in "eskies", so our word isn't the most questionable one for this item.

During those years, people frequently corrected my English. One person used the word "brought" as the past tense of "purchase". Others used the word "bought" as the past tense of the verb "to bring". A locally published scientific paper used the words "must of", where "must have" seemed more appropriate to me.

Was I going mad? Or was English spoken differently in New Zealand from how it had been in my native country? I'm not making excuses, but I *was* born in Birmingham in the West Midlands in the U.K., though I swear I didn't learn to talk until our family moved sixty-five km northeast to relative civilisation.

I use the term *civilisation* loosely here. Look it up.

To make sense of the differences, I enrolled at a community adult education centre within walking distance from the laboratory where I work. I was expelled from the first class. My second teacher set a creative writing assignment. After reading my homework, she too suggested I'd be better off in a different class. That is how I came to submit an application for the Hagley Writers' Institute in Ōtautahi Christchurch.

I was delighted to be offered a place, but soon discovered I had a lot to learn. Not least was a raft of technical features I'd previously not thought about. I hadn't heard of some of them. I'm not referring to grammar, though I had to work at that too. There's only so much you can learn on a part-time course, so I supplemented the classes with reading, scouring the Internet, and paying close attention to feedback offered by more experienced classmates.

I'll only briefly discuss each area related to *word choices* in this chapter, as it's a vast subject. You may wish to read further about some of the topics covered.

Contemporary creative writing utilises carefully selected words. As stressed earlier, reading can help show how language is crafted. You can sense how the written word has evolved through reading literature or non-fiction from different times throughout history. In the twenty-first century, we use fewer of the long sentences favoured a hundred and fifty years ago.

These are generalisations.

Recent publications may deviate from the norm. There's no problem with this, provided the writer considers how words play against each other.

Sometimes modern writing includes incomplete sentences as a stylistic device. Writers may use very long sentences for certain genres, for example, a "single breathless sentence" in flash fiction.

For most styles, using sentences of different lengths works well. Variation keeps your writing lively and interesting.

There has been a shift away from overly descriptive ornate language in the latter part of the twentieth century, sometimes referred to as "purple prose". You've probably come across writing that contains superfluous description, overflowing with excess similes, "thesaurus words" that don't resemble natural speech, plus a soup of adjectives and adverbs.

It's a good idea to pare these back in your writing. Use adjectives and adverbs sparingly in favour of concrete nouns or verbs.

The temptation to use excessive description when introducing a new character, device or world is strong. Sometimes called an "expository lump", this can interfere with the flow of your writing.

Consider the title (if there is one). This is something you might choose before you start a piece, but it's worth reviewing whether it reflects the content as you progress.

Does your work use a narrative hook early on, to draw the reader in?

How does your writing sound? Does it have musicality? Is the rhythm satisfying? How much repetition is there? If present, is it carefully chosen to create a pattern?

Remember to read your work out loud to find clunky spots that don't flow well.

Consider the plot (chain of events) and story elements (factors that drive the narrative: protagonists, conflicts, setting, etc).

Read about story structure. A basic format might start with "world of common day" or status quo, followed by an inciting incident, rising action and resolution. As mentioned in "The (Almost) Infinite Freezer" (chapter one), similar arcs are used in cinema and theatre. I'll elaborate further in "Story Structure" (chapter five), but there are "blueprints" you can follow, including "Freytag's pyramid" and "The Hero's Journey" or "monomyth". These formulae include calls to adventure, testing of characters, escalating tension and awakening or self-discovery. They need not be prescriptive, but can be useful for troubleshooting if your piece isn't working.

Writing can become dull if the pace is too slow. The same thing can happen if heightened action is relentless. Tension and resolution need to be balanced.

Think about point of view (POV). Is your work written in first, second or third person? If third, is it a close third person, which borders on first, or is there more distance? Does only one character's worldview shape the story?

How important is it to be consistent?

You can change perspective, but do so in a considered manner that doesn't suggest, for example, that the author was carried away and forgot they were writing about a fictional character, not themselves. Typically a POV shift takes place between chapters or paragraphs, though I have seen examples of it successfully changing within a sentence.

Omniscient or eye-of-god POV, where multiple characters' perspectives are prominent were more common in the past, but have been used successfully in contemporary literature too.

Think about tense. How important is it to consistently use past, present or future narration within a piece? It isn't, provided the changes enhance rather than appear accidental. For example, changing from past tense to "the dramatic present" can increase the tension of a key event.

Consider how you use association, imagery and symbolism, to suggest concepts rather than describing them directly. Evoking different senses, not only sight, can enhance imagery. Symbolism and imagery work better if not overdone.

*Show don't tell.* Modern narratives allow the reader to work out the full picture without directly spelling everything out.

What would it take to make your story work as a film storyboard or cartoon strip without words? Can you show darkness, for example, by having the character reach out to touch a wall and stepping slowly instead of telling the reader it's dark?

Can a character hear the thud of rain on the roof rather than telling the reader it's raining?

Instead of narrating every inner thought a character has, can you imply them through their responses?

*Show don't tell* can be achieved by using dialogue, but it's not the only way. If direct speech isn't your strength, keep it to a minimum.

Dialogue skills can be improved by eavesdropping on real conversations. Note how people use incomplete sentences, interrupt one another and often use contractions: "don't" rather than "do not", "I'm" rather than "I am". Incorporating consistent verbal ticks can help develop a character, for example, a person who frequently prefaces sentences with, "the truth is", "so" or "well".
Caution: hyper-realistic speech, with the "ums" and "I means" and stuttering can be dull and slow the pace.

Avoid filtering. This is where information presented to the reader is given through the "filter" of a character's response. For example, "I felt Henry was angry." Describe more directly: "Henry was angry." Better still: *describe* Henry's anger through responses the narrator sees. "Henry threw down his towel and bared his teeth."

Avoid unnecessary words, sometimes referred to as "weasel words", although this term does have another meaning that refers to ambiguous claims. Review your text for words such as "just", "almost", "even" and "suddenly". Such modifiers can make the language dull. Is the meaning altered significantly if they're removed? There are more, but these four are common culprits. Train your eye by interrogating them when they appear.

Ernest Hemingway's theory of omission stated: a writer does not need to include everything they know about a subject. If they write well, the reader will get a "feel" for the whole, even if details aren't stated. He uses the analogy of an iceberg:

Essentially, the reader only needs to see the eighth of the entity that sits above the ocean's surface. The writer uses the remaining seven eights of research to ensure the visible eighth appears authentic.

Does your work show a wide range of human emotions?

Clichés can be difficult to identify, because overused words and phrases change with time. Broaden your reading. Good writers will weed "tired" words out. Idioms may come across as overused, although characters might use them in dialogue. Also, they mean different things to different people. "Bob's your uncle" is banned in the laboratory where I work. One staff member's father is called Bob, while another has a brother called Bob. It's confusing.

Dialect is tricky to handle. I've tried emulating my favourite authors in the past, where a character's entire dialogue uses transliterated accented speech. It didn't work as well for me as it did for Irvine Welsh. It's something that's fiendishly difficult to do. It can also come across as offensive, especially if coupled with a stereotypical storyline.

Looking back at my earlier writing, there are elements I wouldn't use now. I'll elaborate in "Respect, and a Question" (chapter seven).

In the previous chapter, I made reference to words people don't like. Some words are deemed "uglier" than others. This is subjective. If you are uncertain about including something, can a thesaurus supply you with a better suggestion? Read the work aloud, ask for critique, or follow suggestions from editors / publishers, who may have "house style" rules regarding no-no words.

Some words appear trashy in close proximity to others. Accidental rhymes can be jarring, as can alliteration. Both can be used to good effect, but typically when they have been chosen with care.

That's plenty of food for thought. It must be time for thoughts about food.

Here's the recipe for this chapter:

## Mirror Glazing

Again, this isn't a recipe, but an activity.

I confess to watching YouTube videos when I'm sick, or using my hands for something else. (Don't ask.) The mirror glazing craze happened in the late twenty-teens. The cover of my first book ("The Crazed Wind", *Truth Serum Press*) features an extreme close-up of a cake that was mirror-glazed by New Zealand artist Deb Williams.

Essentially, you create a high gloss translucent icing that contains chocolate and food colouring and pour a combination of different hues onto a cake that has been covered in an entremet layer, which is essentially a frozen mousse.

It's an extremely fiddly and time-consuming process that's ideal if you're seeking avoidance. See "Writers' Block and What's-the-Pointism" (chapter ten).

This is an example of the ingredients present in a mirror glaze:

## Ingredients

- 15g gelatine powder and 80g cold water (⅓ cup)
- 200g sugar and 100g water
- 200g (⅔ cup) glucose syrup
- 150g (½ cup) sweetened condensed milk
- 200g white chocolate
- food colouring (preferably gel)

## Method

- It would take another chapter to describe what to do, so I suggest you search for "mirror glaze" on YouTube.
- You'll need cream and chocolate (lots of both) for the frozen mousse and a cake to go in the middle. This is an exercise in sheer decadence.

Here's the exercise for this chapter:

## The Time Traveller's Mirror

You don't use a mirror for this exercise, but this title sounded better than "The Time Traveller". Yes, I read it out loud, and checked the rhythm. I don't usually randomly insert words to make a prettier sound, unless I'm writing a song. But the mirror seemed cute after the mirror-glaze icing.

This exercise is inspired by a short story by a well-known New Zealand author that employs a non-linear timeline.

- Your main character is a fugitive. They have been selling anabolic steroids on the underground market. Now they're in prison.
- Write a short piece in three parts, where each section is narrated using a different tense.
- You could start with something that happened in the past, followed by the present, finishing with a scene that will take place in the future. But that's boring. Why not start with the future? Then what? It's up to you.
- Throw in a mirror if you like. Perhaps he or she is selling coke as well. Then I'll be vindicated in choosing the title.
- Complete the first draft of this piece in thirty minutes.

# Chapter Four

## Different Genres

Genre refers to different types of an art form.

Within creative writing, the broader categories include book series, novels, creative non-fiction, standard non-fiction, plays or scripts, short stories, poetry and the short-short form (flash fiction) including novella-in-flash.

There are many sub-categories. It would take a whole book to do them justice. I'm not going to talk, for example, about the *clerihew*, beyond the fact that it's a four-lined poem with an AABB rhyming structure that pokes fun at someone well known.

A novel is a long piece of writing about something made up. Typically, there is a characteristic structure, but more on that later. Incidentally, most of the books in our house are novels. As I'm a slow reader, with a serious novel buying habit, my "to be read" pile could cause an injury if it fell in an earthquake. Excuse the distraction. Let's get back to novels.

How long is a novel? Industry standard is touted as being 80 000 words, and it would be unwise as a new novelist to submit anything that's much longer to an agent or publisher. However, if you consider some classics are over 400 000 words in length, and there are others I'd identify as novel rather than novella, which have less than 30 000, it's clear novels are like the proverbial piece of string. There's a popular children's book series that tops a million words in total.

A novel series is not only a continuation of the same story and cast. The characters generally grow and develop. The voice(s) should be consistent. Each book is complete with a satisfactory ending, but has some dangling threads that can be picked up in the next volume. Read trilogies and series to examine the conventions further if you want to attempt this form.

Script writing is a discipline that specifies the movements and actions of the characters as well as their speech, where inner thoughts are typically revealed indirectly. I would be as likely to attempt screenwriting as to author a manual on how to land a Boeing 737. It would be unwise to attempt either without acquiring the skills first.

Fierce debate surrounds the distinction between literary and commercial fiction. People feel strongly about the merits of each. Lovers of literary fiction have a high regard for the quality of language. These works often tackle "big questions" about the human condition.

Commercial fiction often follows pre-defined formulae and might appeal to a different readership.

Literary journals might exclude what they refer to as genre fiction when seeking submissions. They generally don't publish science fiction, fantasy or romance. Often, these have their own publications and readership.

Poetry is a mystery. It's the most ethereal form of word alchemy. When it comes to poems, I know what I like, and even write them on occasion, but I couldn't critically evaluate one any more than I could read a knitting pattern in Braille.

I haven't defined tanka poems, sonnets, haibun, haiku, pantoums and villanelles. It's best to read examples of these forms if you want to write them. Attend poetry readings to get a better feel of the different categories.

Technical writing is creative in its own way. The flat pack instructions I referred to earlier are innovative, perhaps allegorical, crossing the boundary from practical into surrealism or metafiction.

It would be a lie to pretend I know much about the genres I've mentioned. Although I've written novels, to date the majority of my published work is flash fiction, or a linked series of very short stories known as a novella-in-flash.

Very short fiction goes by many names including flash, short-short, sudden or micro fiction, though the latter may be regarded as a short-short-short form. One subtype, drabble, is composed of exactly 100 words.

The shorter forms are characterised not only by their word count. They use poetic techniques of compression and figurative association. There has been much discussion about the overlap between flash fiction and prose poetry. Some practitioners state there is a distinct difference in both forms. Others view the boundary as blurred.

This style of writing leaves space for the reader's creative response. Not everything is spelled out, though if the writing is too obscure, you may lose the reader.

There are extreme versions of the short-short form such as five-word stories. I haven't yet encountered a one-word story genre.

I've short-changed you in this chapter by telling you what I don't know rather than giving you concrete facts.

In compensation, the recipe is a whole menu. The exercise for this chapter has multiple steps, and includes homework.

Here are the recipes:

## It's Not Only About Cake

Not long after I left the place in the north of England that would ice up inside the windows, I moved to a basement apartment that had a high humidity level. Toadstools sprouted from the carpet, and it took days to dry a towel.

Unemployment was high. My friends and I were looking for work. We'd feed 50p coins into the fuel meters and cook. We used whatever ingredients we had to hand. Not all our meals conformed to an obvious theme.

# Larcomas

If you search for larcoma on the Internet, you're unlikely to find anything that relates to cabbage or potato. That's because the night before we made these cabbage and potato delights, my friend had a dream about excising fist-sized tumours from people's abdomens. The tumours were round and knobbly, and light brown in colour. They were called larcomas.

She told me about her dream as we chopped and mashed, assembled and fried. When the balls we were making came out if the pan, we looked at each other and couldn't stop laughing.

I still refer to these savoury delights by this name forty years on.

## Ingredients

- 10 large outer leaves of a cabbage. Savoy works well
- 4 medium potatoes, boiled and mashed (skin on), approx. 500g
- 2 medium onions, finely chopped
- 3 cloves garlic, crushed
- 2 shallots or 2 spring onions, finely chopped
- 1 tsp salt
- 1 tsp smoked paprika
- ½ tsp turmeric
- ½ tsp ground cinnamon
- ½ tsp nutmeg powder
- a pinch of black pepper
- a pinch of cayenne pepper
- ¼ cup chopped coriander leaves,

- ¼ cup methi (fenugreek) leaves (optional)
- ½ cup gram / chick pea flour (besan)
- ¼ to ½ cup cold water
- salt and freshly ground black pepper to taste
- vegetable oil for frying

## Method

- Make a thin batter by adding sufficient water to the gram flour to create the consistency of thick gravy. Season with salt and pepper.
- Leave to stand while you prepare the other ingredients.
- Boil the cabbage leaves in water until they wilt. Drain.
- Fry the onion, garlic, shallot / spring onion in about 2 tbsp of oil, until they begin to caramelise.
- Add spices, herbs, salt and mashed potato. Continue frying for ten minutes, stirring frequently.
- Add a tablespoon or so of water to the pan if potato mixture sticks. Cool slightly.
- Divide the potato mix into ten equal parts.
- Fill each cabbage leaf with a portion of the mixture and roll into a tight ball.
- Prepare for shallow frying. Heat oil in a pan or wok that can safely contain oil to a depth of 4cm.
- Mix batter well.
- Dip each ball in the batter and fry in batches until batter turns golden.
- Drain on kitchen towel.
- Serve hot with chilli sauce or chutney.

# Blöd's Burgers

Making burgers at home is fiddly, time consuming and cheaper than visiting a fast food outlet; ideal when you have very little money and lots of time. These vegetarian burgers were invented by someone called Blöd, a great cook with a less than complimentary nickname derived from a 1970s U.K. television programme. Blöd is no longer called Blöd, but the burgers live on.

## Ingredients

- 4 slices of wholemeal bread
- zest of half a lemon or lime
- 2 medium onions, finely chopped
- 1 medium carrot, grated
- 1 stick celery, chopped
- 200g mushrooms, wiped and diced
- 4 cloves garlic
- ½ cup almond meal
- 100g strong-flavoured cheese, grated
- 2 eggs, beaten
- ½ tsp salt
- pinch of freshly ground black pepper
- 1tsp dried mixed herbs
- vegetable oil for frying

## Method

- Macerate bread, lemon / lime zest and garlic in food processor to form fine breadcrumbs, and place crumb mix in a large bowl.
- Finely chop onions and sauté in 1 tbsp of oil until golden.
- Add celery, carrot and mushroom. Cook vegetables until softened. Allow to cool a little.
- Meanwhile, stir almond meal, cheese, herbs, salt and pepper into the crumb mix.
- Stir in cooked vegetables and eggs.
- Mix well and form patties approx. 2cm thick.
- Shallow fry in oil until each side is golden.
- Serve with salad and baked potatoes.

## Fruit Crumble Jumble

This recipe is a jumble, because you throw in a mixture of whatever fruit you can find. If it's harvest time, ideally, you'll know someone who has a fruit tree who'll give you a bag of apples, plums or pears. There was an infinitesimally small chance of that happening in the heart of a northern city in the 1980s. So we trawled the City Market, where people sold anything from sausages to sex toys. You'd occasionally get lucky and score a sack of fruit for a fraction of the price you'd pay in the supermarket. Then you'd share your spoils with friends. Someone would return the favour the following week.

## Ingredients

- 1kg of fruit such as apples, pears, plums, peaches, nectarines, rhubarb or berries. (Include canned or frozen fruit if it's off-season)
- 2 slices wholemeal bread food processed into fine breadcrumbs
- ½ tsp ground cinnamon
- ½ tsp ground ginger
- 1 cup oats
- 100g butter, softened
- 2 tbsp brown sugar, more if using tart fruit

## Method

- Preheat oven to 180°C.
- Prepare fruit (peel / core / chop).
- Cook fruit in a pan until soft, adding a few drops of water to prevent flesh from catching and burning. If the fruit is particularly acidic, add enough sugar to make it palatable.
- Pour cooked fruit into ovenproof dish.
- In a large bowl, combine breadcrumbs, oats, spices and sugar.
- Roughly rub the butter into the crumb mix and sprinkle over the fruit.
- Bake for 25 minutes or until crumble topping starts to brown.
- Serve with custard / cream / ice cream / milk.

Here are the exercises for this chapter:

## Crossing the Genre Boundaries

Do you have a favourite genre? Is there a type of writing from the ones listed you have never tried? Or are you a writer who likes to have a go at many different forms?

## Ingredients

- An existing piece of writing: a poem, short story, excerpt from a novel or play, or writing from an earlier exercise.

## Method

## Starter

- Rewrite the piece in a different genre.

## Main course

- Expand the new piece. So, for example, if your scene from a play has become a prose poem, design a small collection of prose poetry

using the new piece as a component. There is no time limit on this. However, for the purpose of the exercise, you don't have to complete all the elements, only work out the structure.
• When planning the bigger version, explore the theme(s) this hypothetical work will cover. Jot down a list of titles for the poems, etc. Are you happy with the order of your table of contents? When you have curated them to your satisfaction, write three of the pieces for homework.

If you converted a piece of flash fiction into a page of a novel, examine what you've done to change it. Have you added characters? Make notes about the characters' lives, including elements you didn't imagine when / if they inhabited the original flash fiction piece.

Write a character study for one of the minor / new characters. How old are they? What is their relationship to the existing character(s)? Where were they born? Do they have siblings? What do they do for a living? Are they a morning or night person? Do they have any distinguishing physical characteristics or verbal tics? Is there anything they refuse to eat?

Using this new information, write the next chapter of the novel. For homework, write a synopsis for the whole novel.

If you started with a poem, convert it into a shopping list or set of instructions, possibly in the style of flat pack assembly instructions. Okay. That might not be a viable option, but the idea is to convert something and then expand it.

## Dessert

- Take a piece of *someone else's* writing and subject it to the same treatment.

I wonder what a paragraph from a gossip column re-done as a chapbook of clerihews would be like ...

# Chapter Five

## Story Structure

Life is chaotic.

Always expect the unexpected.
    Always expect the unexpected.
        Always expect the unexpected.
            Always expect the unexpected.
                The unexpected.

This morning, I was talking with a writer friend about what we're working on. She's completed a family history and is moving on to personal memoir. I told her I was busy too. Several tasks have collided in the *must do now* zone.

I hadn't expected instructions for a structural edit, a copy edit on a different manuscript plus feedback from a sensitivity reader to arrive in my inbox at the same time.

Incidentally, I've written more about what sensitivity readers do in "Respect, and a Question" (chapter seven).

Before the traffic jam of tasks, I'd been storyboarding for a picture book, editing three short pieces before submission deadlines and turning out chapters for *this* book.

Now my partner has broken a bone. I'm on weekend duty at the laboratory and the cat is desperate for attention. Our feline pushes his nose onto my laptop when he's needy. He snaps it closed to clarify my MacBook is his territory, not mine.

Something has to be temporarily shelved, I say to my friend.

She asks what it will be.

The picture book, I reply.

I've been working on "Tigers, Frogs, A Cat and Four Dogs" for six years. It can be delayed for a few more months. The project is the hardest thing I've attempted since I started making books. Stupidly, I aim to create the ingredients myself: characters, raising agent, text, flour, artwork, sugar and cover design.

I must have used a bad recipe.

I've written it in rhyme – a vile delinquent crime, (ouch), unless you've mastered the art of scansion and have a superlative sense of rhythm. Also, as a beginner, illustrating your own work is unwise. Publishers prefer to appoint their own artists. Given I'm not trained as an illustrator, I've spent kilo-hours teaching myself the techniques. At least YouTube provides useful content, apart from mirror glazing vids and instructions for creating series III mechanoids from compound chocolate.

There's design to consider. Design is a necessary component in the armoury of the picture book maker. Those letters don't land on the page and orientate themselves without help. Someone positions them, marries the text and images, advises on structural elements such as the best combination of single and double spreads so pages turn in a sympathetic manner and the story flows well.

It's not easy. You might bake with sugar, but have you tried *making* the sugar?

After updating each other on our writing news, my friend and I lamented how time-consuming everything was. Even writers are prone to clichés: *Can't believe it's August already,* she said. Then we talked about time perception.

It is universally acknowledged that time flows faster from an older person's perspective. I used to think this was because each year constituted a smaller proportion of our lives, until I read that it had something to do with some gland or other. Was it the pituitary, thyroid or prostate? I can't remember, and I've never been able to verify this intriguing fact with a reference.

Incidentally, there are no references in this book, because I can't remember where I first heard the things I've written about. I've tried not to copy anyone's work. If someone holds the copyright to something called a larcoma, I apologise.

My perception of how sluggishly the picture book is progressing doesn't change as I age. It was *painfully* slow six years ago, and still is now. One of the children I tested an early draft on moved onto reading middle grade "chapter books" soon afterwards, and now consumes full-sized novels. Yesterday, she completed a book two-hundred-and-fifty-thousand words in length. (So much for the 80k limit.) She'll be reading to her own children before I finish "Tigers".

My friend and I talked about novels. I told her I hope to start another soon. It's been a while. I will begin on November 2nd. That may seem rather specific, but constraints help me get organised. It's mid-August now, so I have two and a half months to complete everything that's simmering on the word-stove, apart from the picture book, which has been shoved in the word freezer and might remain there another six years.

As well as aiding time management, constraints can focus a wandering mind. A blank sheet with the option of *any* word in the whole lexicon provides too much choice for some. We vacillate without restrictions, even if restraints serve only to send us screaming and running away from the prescribed task.

*I refuse to write a 1000-word story with a helical timeline. I'm doing a poem about rabbits instead. Try stopping me.*

Prompt words help for the same reason. (There are many in the "Extra Exercises" section at the end of this book.)

The human mind is drawn to form. This may be why we evolved conventions around story structure. I touched on this in "Word Choices" (chapter three).

The "consumer" is typically unaware how a well-considered structure underpins a story. Their focus is to enjoy the narrative. Yet if it is not constructed well, the reader or viewer will be dissatisfied, and may abandon the work.

The plot needs areas of high crash-bang-wallop to be balanced by periods of relative calm. Characters follow a path during a story. They often *want* something and show emotional growth as they navigate turning points.

There are conventions. These may be culturally determined, change with time and vary within genres, but there are some useful patterns. I mentioned Freytag's pyramid and the Hero's Journey earlier. There are others, and though I'd like to talk about the Fichtean curve, as it has such a wonderfully frightening name, and "save the cat", as it sounds so sweet, they probably go beyond the scope of this book.

If you have a visual mind, it helps to see the bones of a story as a graph that's shaped like a hill.

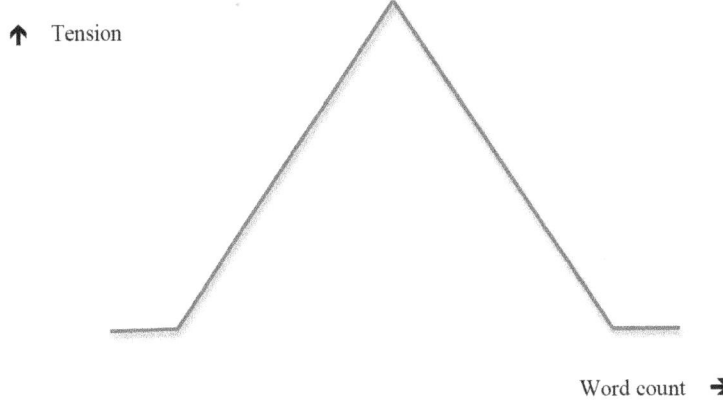

The initial status quo is the horizontal section where the exposition or introductory scene setting happens. An "inciting incident" shifts the curve to an upward trajectory, where tension and drama increase. This event is typically a source of conflict for an important character, though it doesn't have to be conflict in an obvious sense. Perhaps the character realises something important, which in turn affects future actions. The inciting incident is the laxative for the constipation of everyday normality. It gets the plot moving.

Next, the downward slope is where the level of action falls as it heads towards a satisfying conclusion or denouement, when most matters are resolved. Then you reach that flat bit at the end where the reader breathes a sigh of relief.

I referred to the Hero's Journey earlier, which is also known as monomyth, alluding to a concept of a universal story pattern. Twentieth-century American writer Joseph Campbell identified common patterns in myths and stories found throughout the world and compiled an archetype that included elements I mentioned earlier: calls to adventure, testing of characters, escalating tension and awakening or self-discovery. The main character may suffer (abyss or death) before they are enlightened (apotheosis), after which they are homeward bound, ultimately benefitting everyone. It can go the other way too, where a good character turns into a baddie after a negative point in their development.

Not everyone agrees with Campbell's analysis. We probably all know stories that don't subscribe to this pattern. As previously mentioned, templates need not be prescriptive, but can be useful for troubleshooting if something doesn't fall into place. It's good to be aware the models exist, even if we choose to deviate from them, or have little idea how our characters' journeys will end until we complete our work.

Should we worry that following a prescribed formula will make our work predictable? By adhering to monomyth, are we in danger of making monotonous stories?

Probably not.

If you break a story down to its simplest parts, there are only so many tales to be told. Have you ever read a novel blurb on the back of a book, and felt obliged to reconfigure your work in progress because it seems as if it is the same idea? I have. I nearly deleted my novel. In reality, the two are probably very different. Looking at a longer synopsis will reveal this.

Increase the word count further. Perhaps compare the first five paragraphs of each work. Unless you are deliberately plagiarising, or have a troublesomely accurate subliminal memory, you'll discover the unique characteristics of each. Do the maths. The combinations and permutations expand dramatically as you increase the sample size. Going in the other direction, break them down to five or six word summaries, if you consider all the novels ever written in the language throughout history, you'll start to see some duplication, but there's still a high degree of variation. If you head towards that elusive one word story, what's left to write about? Probably lots. There are many words.

Structural edits happen after you think you've nailed it, only to discover event E ought to have happened before B, and character C needs a new uncle. I'll mention more about them in "Other Ingredients for a Book" (chapter twelve). This edit is an opportunity to iron out flaws in story structure. Critique from a second party is useful, as the mentor / editor / assessor may see something the author doesn't. Working closely on a project for prolonged periods coats sections of your work in word glue. They stick in a particular format in your mind. You need a solvent in the form of another person to shift them.

Although only indirectly related to story structure, I'll mention a few other points here. I stated earlier that a piece of writing needs an effective hook near the beginning, or in the back cover blurb, to draw the reader in. One way of examining this is to identify the opening passages of classics or books that have won literary awards. There are some killer first lines around.

Consider what the unifying theme of your work is, and avoid having too many, because that can muddle the structure.

If foreshadowing, be subtle. It's entertaining for the reader to feel they've worked hard to deduce what was hinted at. Too subtle, and foreshadowing serves no purpose. The location of a clue within the narrative acts as a "nudge" to the reader. If there isn't any immediate context for a piece of information, it helps the reader know it's a hint, and prompts them to ask questions. *They've mentioned the vicar smokes a pipe for no apparent reason. Perhaps it's important for later. I'll look out for strands of pipe tobacco.*

Likewise, if subtext or underlying meaning is used, is it clear? Is it subtle enough? Layers of implied meaning beyond the superficial can be very powerful. Subtext can be used, for example to offer social commentary or criticism.

Explore different styles of presenting your work, for example, epistolary, in the style of a letter. In metafiction, a story lies within a story. The narrative voice is that of the author, and they alert the reader to the fact that they are reading a work of fiction.

If you use "authorial intrusion", as I do here, because I'm addressing you directly, it needs to be consistent and in keeping with the overall style of the work.

On to the recipe for this chapter:

## How to Thread a Quilt Cover onto a Duvet

There was a lot of food in the last chapter. In this one I've included a recipe for marital harmony instead.

Like learning how to fold a fitted sheet, "re-sheathing" a duvet is a life skill that should be taught in schools. They could initially train pupils with cot-sized quilts and progress to master classes in super king size. Attaching a quilt cover whose dimensions exceed your arm-span is an Olympic sport as far as I'm concerned.

This isn't an easy thing to describe.

## Method

• Start with the quilt cover *inside out.*
• Feed your arms into the cover, gathering and releasing clumps of fabric until you have a corner in each hand.
• The corners need to be the opposite ones to those that are adjacent to the opening. As the cover is inside out, your hands will be grasping the *right* side of the fabric, but be inside the cloth.
• Next, capture two adjacent corners of the quilt, *through* the cover. Do this lengthwise or width wise, according to the orientation of the cover's opening. You grasp the quilt *through* the cover, so its *wrong* side is in contact with the inner.
• Now comes the hard part. Don't let go of the corners. Grasping them firmly, cast the cover over the body of the quilt, turning it right side out in the process. If you live somewhere with an elevated floor overlooking a lower level over a railing or banister, it's helpful to throw the quilt over the barrier, so you can dangle it downwards. A mezzanine floor or balcony is ideal for this.
• Shake.
• The cover is now right side out, enveloping the quilt. You can safely release the corners you've been gripping and lay the covered quilt on the flat surface of the bed.
• Through the open end, access the other two quilt corners, the ones nearest the opening, and feed them into the corresponding (nearside) corners of the cover.
• Fasten the opening.

• Remember, when taking a dirty cover off, allow it to turn inside out as you remove it, and keep it that way when it is washed and dried, so it's ready to attach. It also reduces colour fading if drying in direct sunlight.

Here's the exercise for this chapter:

## Messing About with Time

Plan a biography about someone you know well. It could be a historical figure, family member or fictional character. The person could be from a book or film, or you can make them up.

Alternatively, work on an autobiography.

## Method

• You don't need to actually write this. Simply construct ten to twenty lines that describe the person's life stages, *but* don't do this in chronological order. For example, you might start with a deathbed scene or their wedding day, and then flash back and forwards to incorporate various stages of their life. Part two will be easier if you date each stage, or make a note of the character's age.
• Copy the list re-organising it so it's in chronological order.
• Review both lists. Do any of the juxtapositions you've made in the non-linear timeline add anything to the story? In what way are they better than the linear timeline, if at all?

This exercise is to examine one element of story structure – the timeline. It can be tempting to write non-linear narratives without giving much thought to why we do it. I am a recidivist time scrambler. In its laziest form, you might add a flashback to "explain" something that's about to happen in the main timeline. This can come across as a contrived afterthought. If you insert the information further back in the narrative, it may instead act as subtle foreshadowing. Word processing makes this simple. If you write long hand, you need a system for inserting modifications, such as taping in extra bits of paper.

Flashbacks and flash forwards can be a poignant way of revealing the storyline, aiding character development in an original way. However, it's wise to *craft* non-linearity so it adds to the reader's experience, rather than jumping back and forth because that's the order in which the ideas come to you.

There's a lot to learn about story structure, and I have only scratched the surface here. Hopefully it provides some direction regarding what else to read about, and changing the bedding might be easier for you now, if that was ever a problem.

As for me, the unexpected has happened again. I might have to re-reschedule my projects. The red-inked edits for another manuscript are likely to be through in a few days. As my friend noted, *Can't believe it's August already.* It's not only that. I can't believe how many things I have to do in August.

Jumping back to my cat, if you'll excuse the non-linearity, he's jumped onto the laptop again. I think he wants to write a story. I could save his attempts and call the folder "save the cat's", rather than "save the cat". After billions of goes, I don't think he'll recreate the complete works of William Shakespeare, but he might manage a ten-letter word.

Wouldn't it be great if that word were "unexpected"?

# Chapter Six

## Sets & Drugs & Rock & Roll & Shady Characters

I need rosemary for tonight's dinner, the herb, not a person. There's plenty of the stuff growing at the old homestead down our road. Walking past earlier today, I pinched several sprigs of it. (That's not all I stole when I was out, but more on the other criminal activity later in the book.)

Back home, I'm washing the stolen goods, when I notice the rosemary leaves are more pliant than expected. And they're hairy. They don't smell like rosemary.

They're not rosemary.

I don't know what they are, but I hope they aren't poisonous. If they are, I've come close to topping off everyone in the house by topping tonight's flat bread with leaves that are not rosemary.

Some botanicals are best not eaten. The seeds, leaves, roots and other bits of many plants are poisonous.

Foxglove, for example, contains digitoxin. As the name suggests, this substance is a toxin. Consuming any part of the plant can make you sick, leading to nausea, visual disturbances, vomiting and diarrhoea. I could tell you what the latter looks like under the microscope – I've worked in medical laboratories for years – but I won't. Unless you're four years old, you're unlikely to be curious about these things.

No doubt you are aware, there's another side to foxglove's personality. The cardiac glycoside drug digoxin derived from the plant, is used for various heart conditions.

Deadly nightshade contains atropine, which can kill you. In controlled amounts atropine is a useful drug during general anaesthesia.

Even shadier is oleander, which is grown for its attractive flowers, but also contains a deadly toxin. It was once believed an extract from the plant could cure snakebite, though this has since been disputed. Oleander is the archetypal baddie pretending to be a goodie when in reality it's a bad guy.

I could go on.

I could tell you about the castor bean and a poison called ricin, and how it was implicated in the death of a Bulgarian dissident in the 1970s and the role of a purported poison umbrella gun, but that goes beyond the scope of this book.

It's good to learn about poisonous plants from a health and safety perspective, but also because they are captivating. Like people, they have nuanced characters.

Inventing characters is one of the most enjoyable aspects of creative writing. You have permission to make imaginary friends, even if you are over the age of four. You can introduce them to a juicy plot, you can bend them, enlighten them, allow them to be loved by unrequited loves, and then you can kill them.

Character creation isn't confined to fiction. In non-fiction too, the author only shows aspects of the person they write about that they want the reader to know. They may choose to lie by omission.

I'll let you in on a secret. I'm not really writing this book. Someone else is. I didn't steal anything from them despite my kleptomaniac tendencies. They gave me their name and the words, but created a persona to address you. They are way more boring than I am, so they needed me to do this.

Maybe you do something similar yourself. Do you have a social media presence? Apparently it's a good idea for writers to promote their work and connect with their readers via the world of Xstabooktok or whatever it's called. But do you show your true self? Or are you demonstrating a lighter side? Or perhaps you're portraying a darker one.

Do you remember the shock rock musicians from the 1970s? I was surprised, perhaps a little disappointed, to discover the hedonistic bad guys we idolised as teenagers turned out to be church-going, golf-playing, respectable citizens. They were more like our parents than us. They were more like the people who despised them for their on stage bat-biting, chicken-murdering antics. These musicians presented a persona while performing. At home they probably mowed their lawns and cleaned their cars like you and I do. (Actually that's a lie. I've rarely done either of those things.)

How much thought do we need to put into making the characters we write? It can be fun to allow our pretend-people to grow naturally without contriving every feature. But it's useful to check them early in their creation, to get to *know* who they are.

Make your characters memorable. Make them complicated. Take charge of their development. Typically a character arc, particularly in a novel, will show a change of some sort in the person. In the previous chapter, I mentioned all characters should *want* something. They may not know *what* they want, but they yearn for something. Achieving or gaining that thing may bring about the change, or the character might develop because they *don't* find what they thought they wanted.

Perfect characters don't make for good stories. Readers are drawn to flaws, whether in the primary character or supporting cast. People are boring if they lack any foibles. Possessing faults also allows for redemption when characters reach turning points.

Making your characters likeable in spite of their defects is effective. The reader is more likely to invest emotion in the person and will want to discover what happens to them if they care about them.

As you make your goodies a little bit bad, take care to make your baddies a little bit good too. They will be far more compelling and memorable.

Are all your characters similar to yourself? You might not think so, but even your villains can be replicas of you. It took years for me to realise all my characters were atheists, like me. Even the ones labelled as religious. I gave them churches, synagogues, mosques or temples to attend, but I didn't leave my mind and enter theirs to perceive and then show how they saw the world with a god(s) in it.

If you identify with a certain ethnic background, for example European, do you automatically create European characters as standard? Are the non-Europeans playing tokenistic roles? The same applies for any minority groups, such as gay characters, those with disabilities or people who crochet. Do you make too much of their differences?

*Look. Here's someone in a wheelchair. Notice them, please.*

Or can they simply exist, as minorities do in real life? Work the subtleties of the wheelchair user's movements into the fabric on the text without fanfare, and the writing will appear more realistic, rather than creating the impression they have been squeezed in to make up the numbers of lesbians / people with disabilities / crochet enthusiasts.

Be careful when writing outside your own experience. Research carefully and seek feedback. I'll touch upon this again in "Respect, and a Question" (chapter seven).


There may be one or more main characters or protagonists in a story. These individuals don't have to be introduced at the very beginning. Lesser characters instead might be pushed into the foreground as other story elements such as setting and style are established.

Secondary characters may have a major role, for example as antagonist.

Less important characters lack a critical role, but help establish the ordinary world more central figures inhabit.

Characters' roles can change through the piece.

When a minor character is given a point of view, i.e. the narrative comes from their perspective, whether that is in first or third or even second person, they cross a line and can be considered a protagonist, though the boundary can be blurred. The reader may be exposed to the character's inner thoughts directly, or they might comprehend the individual's introspection through their actions. Either way, the reader is being invited to identify with that character.

As you consider the interplay between major and minor characters, assess whether they are all necessary. Too many characters can cause confusion and the reader may lose interest or miss the significance of a key action carried out by one of many people.

Characters' physical appearance and verbal tics can help show their individuality. It can be tempting to attach too much significance to physical appearance in the early stages of a piece. Rather than providing too much data when the character is introduced (an expository lump), it is more effective to distribute detail throughout the narrative. Take particular care regarding appearance when writing in first person. Characters need a reason to mention a physical trait.

*I ran my fingers through my blonde curly hair.*

Why are they saying this? Is it purely for the benefit of the reader? Give them a reason to introduce physicality.

*I always wondered why my hair was blonde and curly when the rest of the family had straight brown hair.*

*I envy Karen's auburn hair. I feel like a bimbo next to her with my blonde curls.*

*My bush is black and frizzy in contrast to the blonde curls on my head. Why are pubes so contrary?*

Choose your characters' names with care. Are they correct for the location, era and class? Are there too many main characters with names beginning with the same letter that the reader may confuse? For the same reason, it's a good idea not to have characters that are very similar in any other way, unless that's a deliberate feature of the story.

Do you use abbreviated versions of characters' names? If this is not done consistently, is there a reason?

Not all characters are people. Apart from non-human animals, these include personifications or abstract concepts. You may have heard the town or city in a story described as a character when it evokes a strong sense of place. We'll consider more about setting later in this chapter.

It's a good idea to keep a character list as you develop your work. Record their features and be consistent – unless you deliberately make a character behave in an uncharacteristic matter, which can be quite powerful, especially if it is foreshadowed.

You may include in-depth character studies in these notes. What sort of school did the person attend? How many siblings did they have? Did their parents divorce? What careers have they had? What is their accent? What is their attitude towards money? Can they drive? Are they ill? Do they tell lies?

Using unreliable characters can add depth to a story.

Have fun. These are your people.

I started the chapter title with "sets", but the "setting" section is tucked away after the other stuff. "Drugs & Rock & Roll & Shady Characters & Sets" would have been a lame title, so forgive me.

Setting includes time, place, and other elements that provide a base for your narrative. As with protagonists, setting doesn't have to be introduced immediately, though it probably needs to be established reasonably early.

I mentioned the *expository lump* earlier in the context of character, i.e. overloading the reader with excessive undiluted description. The same applies when introducing your setting. It's better to create the characters' world as an integral part of the storytelling than to dump too much description at the outset.

Consider the period in history when your story takes place. What signposts can you use to determine or reinforce this? How does the era influence the choice of language, both in dialogue and reported speech? How are characters' attitudes influenced by the *when?* What about gender roles? Ideas about race? How does social stratification impact on your characters? What technology is prevalent? For example, is much of the lighting after nightfall from candles, lamps and fireplaces? What sort of transport do people use in that era?

If you're creating a fantasy world, what parallels are there with real history?

What is the duration of the narrative? Consider what changes are required to show time progressing in the story, for example shadow lengths, the passage of seasons, evolution of cell phones, or changes in life expectancy.

Factor in the weather for the climate of the location. Consider length of daylight and moon phases. For example, don't have a full moon two weeks after the last full moon. If you are writing non-fiction or realistic fiction, you might check what the weather was like in a particular place when a historical event took place. Evoke all the senses so a reader experiences the setting along with the characters. Fragrances and odours can be particularly useful for this.

Pace is important. How does the rate at which time is covered vary from page to page, or chapter to chapter? Some parts of a story warrant being conveyed in more detail than others, but if the writing becomes laboured and sluggish it will interrupt the flow and you may lose your reader.

I touched on timelines in "Story Structure" (chapter five). When you read books or watch film and theatre, observe how time is handled. As well as linear versus non-linear timelines, one character's timeline may be handled differently from another's. Consider why these choices have been made. If you play around with timelines (a necessity if writing about time travel, for instance), keep detailed notes to avoid unplanned conundrums.

*Where* is your narrative taking place? Are there multiple locations? How are the senses evoked as your characters move through the space you have provided for them? When you describe locations, you can draw on real places you have visited. Use your catalogue of memories. Travel diaries are useful. You can transplant details from one real place to another and invent a new imagined scene.

Compared with writers in the past, we have the benefit of online satellite images. Drop in and explore a place you've chosen to write about, even if you've already been there in real life. Use the delicious details available.

Video clips from a chosen destination can help you describe sounds in an authentic manner. You can't actually smell what the inhabitants can, but look at visual detail, and let your imagination fill in the rest for the reader's benefit. Do those cages full of chickens emit a meaty odour with sour high notes? Can you sense the damp earth on that forest floor? Is there a whiff of fungus under those leaves?

Imagination is an essential tool, especially when you don't have reference material. What does that alien's skin feel like? How is vision affected when light doesn't travel in straight lines? Has that corpse been there long enough to reek?

An elusive component of setting is *what's happening in their world?* For example, do the events take place against a backdrop of a war or other conflict? Are your characters potentially affected by an acute water shortage? Is there a pandemic that shapes the characters' responses and choices? When you consider aspects of your characters' worlds that shape their opinions and potentially influence their actions, you'll write them convincingly with more empathy.

Here's the recipe for this chapter:

## Flat Bread with Chia Seeds and Rosemary

I suppose you saw this coming. Try not to poison yourselves.

## Ingredients

- 2 cups high-grade flour plus more for shaping the dough
- 2 tsp dried yeast
- 1 cup tepid water
- 2 tsp sugar
- ½ tsp salt
- 2-4 tsp olive oil
- 1 tbsp fresh rosemary leaves roughly chopped
- 1 tbsp chia seeds

## Method

- Mix two cups flour, the sugar and salt in a large bowl with a whisk.
- Add the yeast and water and mix well with a fork. It will be sticky.
- Cover and leave in a warm place for one hour.
- Line a baking sheet with greaseproof paper and sprinkle generously with flour.
- Spoon the risen dough onto the floured surface, sprinkle more flour on top, and shape into an oval 1-2cm thick. Cover and leave in a warm place to rise. After thirty minutes, set oven to preheat at 240°C, allowing bread to rise for ten further minutes while the oven reaches temperature.
- Bash out some crosshatched lines 5cm apart across the dough with a wooden spoon.
- Brush bread with oil.
- Sprinkle with rosemary leaves and chia seeds, pushing them into the dough.

• Bake for seven to nine minutes, until bread sounds "hollow" when tapped with wooden spoon.

This bread is good with hummus. *But you didn't say when to knead it,* I hear you ask. You don't need to knead it. That's why I like this recipe. I like shortcuts. Unfortunately, there aren't any shortcuts when it comes to sculpting your characters and settings with care.

Here's the exercise for this chapter:

## Who am I?
## Where am I?
## When am I?

You can carry out this exercise using a character from a work in progress. Otherwise create someone new. When I suggested making character lists earlier in the chapter, I noted a few features:
• Schooling
• Siblings
• Parental relationships
• Career
• Accent
• Finance
• Transport
• Health
• Integrity

Expand this list, adding three more parameters needed to define a person.

Now complete the full list for your chosen character. If you have just created them, give some thought to the scenario they will be placed in. You can invent a situation, or choose from the following:
• A character tries to poison their spouse.
• Espionage story, where the protagonist has been commissioned to eliminate a target, OR the character is a potential target.
• A fan discovers their rock star hero isn't who they thought they were.

Write for ten minutes, featuring the character you've outlined. If it's someone from your work in progress, you might use the piece, or it may become an unseen story that never makes it into the final work, but will help you know the character better.
    Now rewrite the story, setting it a hundred years before or after the original time setting, taking a further ten minutes to do this.


There's a lot to learn about characterisation and creating engaging settings. Though we have only skimmed over the basics, hopefully it provides you with some pointers for further reading.

# Chapter Seven

## Respect, and a Question

A colleague and I were discussing our addictions today. We both suffer from the same affliction. It's a disease, not a crime I feel, and should be managed through education and counselling, rather than censure and condemnation.

We need help.

Without support, we could harm our loved ones as we syphon big bucks away to fund our habit. Desperate to satisfy our cravings, my workmate and I might blow part of the grocery budget on stimulants, and our families will go hungry as a result. Potentially addicts can incur massive debts, risking losing the roof over their heads. They could eventually resort to crime to feed their depravity.

Some of the commodities we crave have electronic equivalents. Think of them as being akin to e-cigarettes. There are advantages to choosing this route, but many aficionados miss the smell and feel of the real thing.

Some users cut costs by sharing their hardware, but deep down they know it's a mug's game. The practice is not without risk. Sharing can spread infectious diseases. If you must do it, take precautions. Never share with anyone who picks their nose or with people who like beetroot for lunch.

It's a risky deal.

The pushers don't like us sharing. It eats into their profits. They have bills to pay. Overheads. They need to recover the cost of their investments. Though given some cartels run retail establishments in most major cities in the world, they're probably doing all right. The industry proliferates at clubs and festivals, where repeat offenders like myself congregate, often purchasing in bulk.

Commercial outlets for these goods operate in plain sight. I've seen police officers pass them without pausing to investigate, though recently I spotted a copper go inside and come out with a car magazine.

Magazines are a gateway drug leading to addictions of the multi-paged variety (books) or worse. The law enforcer in question will likely progress to the complete works of the presenters of *Top Gear* in two shakes, I fear. Measure for measure, a magazine provides fewer words per buck, so I'm not making much ado about nothing here.

As for my workmate and I, we have slightly different tastes from the petrol-head po-po mentioned above, but she has been known to buy up to three books in one transaction. Of course, I'd *never* do that. I also occasionally tell lies.


I wonder if we're doing the right thing by making more books. Would publishers do the world a favour if they didn't produce so many tomes every year? Bibliophiles' shelves would be less likely to sag and collapse if there were fewer new releases to tempt us – I mean, *them*. If there weren't as many fresh titles to lure their magpie-eyes, they might eventually catch up with their elusive "to be read" piles. These piles can grow to monstrous dimensions and are unresponsive to haemorrhoid creams.

Okay. I'm taking the piss. That's all right within reason. There's nothing wrong with self-deprecating comments, but extending commentary to a whole group isn't so good. If I'd said all medical laboratory workers are addicts, it would be untrue and offensive.

There's a type of discrimination people might excuse – making negative remarks about a cohort you identify with yourself. I used to do this to get cheap laughs, until the day an Indian doctor walked into the lab while I was spinning a yarn that ended with me berating Indians for our obsession with bureaucracy. I use *berating* euphemistically, because the words I actually used were a bit rude.

I'll never forget the expression on that person's face.

It was even worse when I took the mickey (sorry) out of Irish people, because I considered myself Irish through marriage. *I* saw the connection. Others didn't. I've stopped doing that as well.

Generalisations aren't funny. Stereotypes are tiresome. We've probably all encountered writing by people who churn out clichéd bigotry without apparent thought. You don't want to be that person. Even if you only have a limited readership, if a large number of writers reinforce concepts that propagate bias against (or towards) certain groups, we are not serving our readers in the best way possible.

Awareness regarding these issues has increased in recent times. I've written pieces in the past that I'd be wary about penning now. For example, I gave people who spoke English as a second language stilted dialogue with consistently incorrect grammar. I didn't consider how a reader from the region would feel when reading it.

Dialects *can* be used successfully – many writers make very effective use of vernacular – but it's hard to do well. I mentioned this in "Word Choices" (chapter three). It's advisable to check whether you're reinforcing a stereotype if you elect to do this.

Question what drives you to use marked regional accents. I've previously made the mistake of writing characters who face deprivation, or ones who are a "bit thick" with an accent that is far removed from Received Pronunciation, or whatever is seen as standard in a region. There's probably little correlation between low intelligence and a non-standard accent in the twenty-first century.

I'm not saying people from certain backgrounds *never* face deprivation, or that they can't be dim. An analogy is in film and television. While directors wisely increase the presence of actors from minority groups in high profile roles, it would be unrealistic to *never* cast them as villains, and probably discriminatory if they really wanted the job.

A character's "voice" may follow a certain stereotype, and you may need to use a particular dialect because it would sound inauthentic to use neutral diction. However, it's wise to consider whether you have tripped into a trope. Is the approach the best way to convey the narrative? Or have you made lazy assumptions?

If it's inoffensive and necessary for building your character, go ahead. But there are grey areas between acceptable, slightly dodgy and downright rude. The boundaries are subjective. Seek critique from another writer if you're not sure. Seek it anyway. They may see something you don't.

We attempt to eliminate discrimination out of respect for humanity. That doesn't mean your *characters* can't disrespect, show bias against or favour certain groups themselves, but the underlying author's voice should demonstrate some distance from the invented person's perspective.

Don't shy away from making offensive characters. After all, if your protagonist can commit murder, they can also select someone for a position of employment based on shoe or bra size, they can tell someone to stay in the kitchen because of their gender, or maim a person because of their sexuality. Readers love to hate characters' flaws, and enjoy seeing them receive their just deserts.


Is pinching content from other people's lives disrespectful? As writers, we're constantly observing humans in the wild to spark ideas for character traits, sources of conflict, mannerisms and physical appearance, etc.

In the mainstream media there have been several "biopic" films and television series based on real people's lives, where part of the storyline is fictionalised. While that makes for a far more interesting viewing experience, it's not without risk. The same applies to writing at any level.

Unless you have the person's express permission to write in a biographic or semi-biographic manner, or you're deliberately being a grade one prick (this is a particular genre), only use excerpts from people's lives in fiction, and even then, "process" the information. I mean *process* in the way a kitchen gadget would process something: chop it into tiny fragments, mix it up, and make it into something it wasn't before.

This is imperative when writing about the sensitive stuff: how someone wet the bed in their boyfriend's parents' house, were cuckolded by their brother, stole from their mother's purse or is sexually aroused by marmosets.

But if someone has given you permission to write about what they did with their penis last summer, go for it. (I offer grateful thanks to John XY for sharing his experiences, which I have used in another book.)

Stealing someone's sensitive story without permission is rude. Consider how you would feel if it happened to you. It's not enough to change the names. I learned this the hard way. I'm very sorry to the person concerned. You know who you are.

And Francine YZ, (name changed to protect the innocent), don't worry; I will never use what we did in our teens in a story. However, I may have accidentally mentioned it at a party a few years back. I don't think your husband heard. If he did, I'm sorry.

And don't assume your old friends will never read your stuff. I learned that the hard way, too.

Families and writing don't mix well. This is a minefield, and likely to lead to disrespect or death. Be very careful if you're writing about them while they're alive.

I used to hate the fact that few immediate family members read my books. For years, I complained to anyone who'd listen. Now I think it's a good thing. I don't listen to minute details about sports or music they are enthusiastic about, so why should they be interested in my books?

That doesn't mean they will *never* stumble across my work, so I don't have carte blanche to write anything I want about them. I hope my offspring, K and K, forgive me for "I don't go to nursery", and "nomonnit" in chapter two, if they ever read this.

It's not generally recommended that you seek critique from family members. They won't be looking for the things you need to put more work into. There are exceptions. One of my Ks has written film scripts, and understands story structure, so I've requested critique from him in the past.

I mentioned writing about characters that fall outside our own experience in the previous chapter. There's much discussion in the media regarding the rights and wrongs of cultural appropriation, or stealing other people's culture in the arts. It goes beyond the scope of this book to discuss what we should and shouldn't write about people who are "not us".

As a general guide, if you create a character you don't share much cultural background with, do your research. Treat risky topics with respect. Then request a sensitivity reading from someone who has a connection.

I'm forever grateful to a fellow New Zealand writer who provided feedback on a historical fiction book I wrote featuring some Māori characters. I had no idea how far off the mark I was until they gave me some insight into the Māori perspective. This was despite my having researched for hours in the library and online. One character's perspective on fate, the role of deities, ancestry and curses lay beyond my experience, and I needed the other writer's input for authenticity.

Using literal translations of non-English words doesn't always work. Those entities may not be used in the same way as they are from a European viewpoint.

I was asked to give feedback from an Indian perspective to another New Zealand author. At the outset, I outlined my limitations. My worldview is shaped differently from that of the protagonist: a third generation New Zealander of Indian origin, because that's not my experience. (I'm first generation U.K. to Indian parents.)

Cultural appropriation with its assumptions about dominant versus minority cultures is a complex topic. The negative impacts of colonisation need to be recognised and addressed. I respect the wishes of entire groups who want to retain elements of their culture within their own community, especially if they are being diminished or distorted in the hands of others. However, I wonder whether the good intentions behind these objectives are fully understood by many. Have we shifted our focus onto the minutiae when borrowing language, costumes, dance, music and art, rather than understanding how and why cultural theft has a destructive effect?

I appreciate someone drunkenly prancing about in "fancy dress" interpretations of indigenous costumes is not respecting culture. They will reduce the *mana* or prestige of the attire. However, I'm not certain telling my Irish wife of European descent she shouldn't wear a sari to our part-Indian daughter's wedding will ameliorate injustice from past generations.

Categorising what group(s) an individual belongs to is complicated. I have several questions about the process:
• Where do people of mixed race or those who have a legitimate claim to more than one culture fit in?
• How are people whose culture doesn't match their biological features expected to identify?
• How do you categorise people who have rejected or been separated from their culture?
• Does everyone labelled as belonging to a dominant culture have an attitude that reflects the dominant zeitgeist?

• Should we ignore the views of people from so-called minority groups who *want* their customs and practices to be accessible to cultural exchange?
• How narrowly should an individual be characterised when determining which cultures they can legitimately appropriate?

When it comes to writing, should we only create protagonists who are similar to us? Ultimately, should we only write about ourselves?

I end this chapter by posing the question: "Can black bisexuals with back issues only write about black bisexuals with back issues?"

We'll consider the answer to this question in some depth in the next chapter.

Meanwhile, here is the recipe for this one:

## Making a Book – Literally

How many other saddoes tried making books out of scrap paper, string and staples when you were a kid? Perhaps you mass-produced them, photocopying a series of ten or twelve to circulate to friends as you launched your publishing career.

For some, this may be the closest we've come to understanding the process of actually *making* a book. However, bookbinding by hand is a fascinating craft. If you want to "grow your own", having insight about the process is useful. Some literary journals have released very attractive hand-bound issues.

## Ingredients and Tools

- paper for pages
- marbled end papers to line board covers
- bookbinder's paste (a "padding compound" that is flexible yet strong when dry)
- hemp / cotton tape
- Irish three cord linen thread
- buckram / bookbinder's mull – open-weave stiffened muslin to strengthen the spine
- book cloth – a canvas-like fabric for covering cardboard in hardback books
- card – *Formacoat Manilla* – for making curved spines
- cardboard for cover boards
- cobbler's knife
- coping saw
- leather needle
- book press
- drill press

## Method

Enrol in a bookbinding class if you want to do this properly. You can learn the difference between full and open-style spines, and the complex process of pressing collections of pages (quires) together before sawing angled grooves into the bound side that you loop thread through as you sew the paper bundles together.

Here's the exercise for this chapter:

## **Dirty Writing**

• Scour newspaper articles, magazines, non-fiction and fiction for snippets where a minority or oppressed group is not treated with respect.
• Copy key quotes from them.
• Write a short piece or poem featuring some of the quotes.
• Use repetition to enhance the rhythm to increase the impact of the words.

# Chapter Eight

## The Answer to the Question

No.

Here's the recipe for this chapter:

**Nothing**

There isn't one.
It's a public holiday here.
I'm having a day off.

And the exercise:

# Zilch

No homework either.

You have a day off, too.

In case I haven't stressed the importance of good time management enough, take this opportunity to do something else, and return refreshed.

(There are extra exercises at the end of the book if you're desperate.)

# Chapter Nine

## Getting Your Work Out There

I'm meeting a writer friend for dinner for her birthday. Between now and then, I'll obsess about the delicious options on the restaurant's menu. I'm vacillating between roasted cauliflower with cashew cream served with winter slaw, and a rather more decadent combination of marinated anchovies on sourdough followed by confit duck leg with cavolo neros. I understand the latter is a fancy form of kale. I'll finish with tarte Tatin and vanilla bean ice cream.

I've also been fantasising about items that aren't on the menu – a spiced lamb stew, perhaps served with sautéed potatoes or couscous – and maybe a dessert that hasn't been invented yet that tastes like the sky.

I have known this friend for decades. She's written in many genres, and has recently taken up script writing – a very different discipline from producing novels or short stories. I look forward to hearing about the film she's making with her team. It's fascinating to discover more about a process I know little about.

Another writer friend is joining us. This author has written award-winning fantasy books that have been marketed in New Zealand and overseas. She gave a talk on finding an agent when I attended the Hagley Writers' Institute many years ago. I remember her telling us not to be concerned that an agent takes a percentage of the royalties from a book. If you didn't want to lose that portion, she said, you could give it a go on your own and enjoy the full 100%, but of a smaller income.

At writing school, we weren't only taught how to mould ideas; we were also taught to revise our work, taking it to a publishable standard. Then we were given guidance on how to submit to suitable places, including warnings on how to identify "vanity presses", organisations that take payment from authors to make a book. These people have little incentive to get work out to readers, because they've already received their income from the writer.

I was clueless about the publication process prior to attending these classes. Remember, I'd only applied to HWI in order to learn to write the language the way the locals do.

As a teenager, I imagined your work would be "discovered", and then you'd be on a path to having your book in every bookshop in the country. It was rather like a common fantasy kids at my school had about winning big bucks on the football pools – only we never actually took part in any lotteries, as we were too young. We just expected it might *happen,* and talked amongst ourselves about how we'd spend the money. Similarly, our unpolished, first draft "novels" were going to find homes without us sending them anywhere, we believed.

Actually, I thought I *had* been discovered when I was fourteen. A friend showed one of my creations to a publisher her sister knew. This person made a show of being impressed by my story.

A week later, they told me the publisher wanted to release a collection of my work. I gave the matter some consideration, and decided I didn't want to proceed, because I didn't want my dad reading the stuff. Some of it was quite risqué. Well, at fourteen we thought it was. Anyway, it turns out the whole thing was a ruse, and they had a great laugh about it, while I was bemused, wondering why someone would make something like that up.

Writing doesn't simply *get published*. You have to make it happen.

In "A Blind Salesman Moment" (the prologue), I talked about selling your "product", and asked if you felt your writing was marketable. I alluded to the question of whom you were writing for. While it is quite acceptable to keep your writing to yourself and never show your work to anyone, a large number of authors want people to read their creations. I also said it was all right to dream. It's **okay** to want to get your work "out there". We put considerable effort into our short stories, poetry and novels, and it can feel quite isolating to think no one will read them.

Since the advent of the Internet, online journals have flourished, in addition to print publications. Both types include some that pay contributing authors and others that don't. Many have established excellent reputations, attracting work from high calibre writers around the world.

They're not difficult to find. For example, if you are a flash fiction writer, there are several well-subscribed social media groups that showcase work from a range of journals. As I'll discuss further in "The Writing Community" (chapter eleven), these groups provide a great source of camaraderie. They're an excellent way to find publications to submit to, as authors share links to accepted work on these forums.

Some editors offer feedback. Even if they don't, there's much to be learned from reading what has made the grade. Some publications are behind a pay wall, while other online journals are free to read. Some take free submissions, while others require a reading fee. There are sites online that publish lists of journals that will pay for your work, if that is a priority. Expect that you will face stiffer competition when submitting to these. The same applies for those publications that have acquired a reputation for excellence.

It's wise to keep a folder of up to date biographical data (bios). I keep at least four baseline bios: one shorter and one longer version each for local and international submissions. When asked for a bio, I copy a version that's closest to the requirements and modify it to fit the tone of the editorship and cut or expand to the required word count. Mention single author collections, novels, competition successes or acceptances in high profile journals, rather than producing a list of everything you've ever had published. Then, as I mentioned in "The (Almost) Infinite Freezer" (chapter one), archive rather than discard it, because you might base another bio on the format in future.

In the same chapter I mentioned author websites and social media. Although maintaining these can be time consuming, they're useful if a reader wishes to access more of an author's work or potential publishers need to learn more about an author's experience and accomplishments. Remember to update details on directories held by professional bodies you join, such as national Societies of Authors or Writers' Associations.

I also mentioned CVs and "housekeeping" in "The (Almost) Infinite Freezer".

If you're not sure about whether to send your work out, ask for critique. When you've made your piece the best it can be, send it out. I'll discuss feedback further in "The Writing Community" (chapter eleven).

People enjoy reading.

Reading material has to come from somewhere.

If new writers don't hone their skills and promote their writing, where will tomorrow's stories come from?

I talked about the need for a system to keep track of submissions in "The (Almost) Infinite Freezer" (chapter one). Keep folders of your work organised and up to date.

You could regard sending out your work as an apprenticeship. It can be demoralising receiving multiple rejections, especially if you receive many in quick succession. However, those pieces can be re-worked and submitted again. Redrafting your writing effectively is one of the most important skills you can acquire.

I mentioned earlier that longer-form works, such as novels, are harder to place. Unsurprisingly, publishers need more time to read a larger number of words. There may not be an income stream to pay editors for reading time. Therefore, they often don't take unsolicited novel submissions, because they don't want to take a load of potentially unusable work home with them. This can be tough for writers who are looking to publish their first novel.

There are occasional competitions where you can submit novels and gain exposure if your work is short or long listed, but generally it is difficult to get started. It's not an entirely fair process. Some renowned authors who already have a metaphorical foot through the door might publish novels containing plot holes and implausible characters or motivations. However, they have earned their reputation, and their work will sell despite the occasional flaw. Publishers are running a business. They don't exist purely to promote our writing careers.

Supportive friends and family may encourage you with anecdotes about how such-and-such author submitted their novel to fifty publishers before their best-seller was picked up. Non-writers don't realise the system doesn't work that way anymore. There may only be a handful of (usually small) publishers who look at unsolicited submissions from authors who've not had a novel published before.

Having an agent opens some doors, but you require determination and a certain amount of luck to secure one of those. There are conventions regarding how to send query letters to agents. There's more on that subject later in this chapter.

Once you have your work published, whether it is a novel with a mainstream publisher or a short piece on someone's website, you need to promote it. Often this requires a collaborative approach between the publisher and author.

Marketing and promotion don't come for free. This is one of the major differences between mainstream and independent publishers. Massive multi-national companies have a marketing budget and sales team, which they employ for some of their publications. The author will still be required to work with their publicist, perhaps by providing a social media presence, interacting with their readers and attending promotional events. However, every unit sold isn't dependent on their having nurtured a relationship with a potential reader. Plus, there will likely be experienced team members in the organisation who can help plan interviews and readings.

Independent publishers provide an excellent service, but the boss at your day job needn't worry you'll hand in your notice any time soon. Boutique organisations operate on a different scale from the larger publishers. The author needs to interact with friends and family to promote their work, because they aren't going to have their books advertised on billboards, television or on the back of buses.

I've spoken to authors who find this "self-promotion" excruciating. However, a small publisher has typically put in as much effort as a larger one in bringing the author's work to publishable standard. See more on this in "Other Ingredients for a Book" (chapter twelve). This is a partnership, and it's helpful if the author plays a part in getting the book "out there".

Book launches take effort to organise, but they can be rewarding. Launches are a good way of promoting a new title, irrespective of the number of units sold at the event. I cannot stress enough how important the role of cake is. It can provide a focal point, and lure people in off the streets, some of whom may buy a book. I'll elaborate on this in "Where to Next" (chapter fourteen).

It's not cake, but here's the recipe for this chapter:

## Moroccan Lamb Tagine

The craving for lamb stew didn't abate, even though I opted for the cauliflower at dinner. However, obsessing reminded me of the first time I tasted a lamb tagine. Though the food was exquisite, the experience wasn't altogether positive. The travel diary from that trip provided source material for several stories, not all of which are pleasant.

In the mid-eighties, a friend and I went to Morocco. We had a challenging time.

My friend and I arrived in Tangiers after a traumatic ferry crossing. A tout led us to an obscure part of the souk and conned us into purchasing an overpriced carpet. Later, my friend had a nightmare and reached across from the adjacent bunk and pulled my hair. I woke up screaming and scared the crap out of everyone in the bunkroom.

During an aborted attempt to climb Mount Toubkal, my friend was affected by altitude sickness, and ran away. I eventually found her, but we became separated from our guides and the mules that were carrying our gear.

Near Marrakesh one night, a boy crept into the bedroom where a group of us were staying and tried to get into a woman's pants.

I had the most insane stomach upset I've ever experienced after eating prickly pear fruit. My bowels have never been the same since, but it didn't stop me trying the lamb tagine served by a family we stayed with in a small village near the mountains.

I can see this is probably not the most appetising introduction to this wonderful dish.

I hope you enjoy it all the same.

## Ingredients

- 1kg shoulder or leg of lamb cut into small pieces (3-5cm)
- 500g fresh tomatoes
- 500g okra, topped and tailed

- 200g fresh green beans, topped and tailed
- 1 small squash, e.g. butternut, or sweet potato chopped into 2cm cubes
- 3 onions, chopped into 1cm cubes
- 3 cloves garlic, crushed
- ¼ tsp chilli powder
- 1 tsp turmeric
- 2 tbsp olive oil
- 1 tsp salt, plus more to taste
- warm water to cover

## Method

- Mix meat, onions, garlic, spices, salt and oil in a large pan.
- Cover with warm water and bring to the boil.
- Cover and simmer until meat starts to soften (approx. 1 to 1½ hours, depending on cut).
- Meanwhile, prod whole tomatoes with a fork and hold over gas flame, if you have one, until skin begins to pop. Alternatively, plunge tomatoes into boiling water for one minute. Peel and roughly chop.
- Add all vegetables to the stew, cover and cook until meat and veg are tender (approx. 1 further hour).
- Adjust seasoning to taste.
- Serve with couscous or tortilla wraps.

Here's the exercise for this chapter:

# Elevator Pitch

You're tired after attending a million talks at the country's largest literary festival. You've met a ton of friends, some of whom you only knew through social media before; plus you've been introduced to a whole load of new ones.

It's a twenty-minute walk between the venue and the place where you're staying, and you go back and forth several times a day. Your back pack contains your laptop, a bottle of water, and another new book or two every time you leave the festival site, and it really is a bad time for that mysterious back pain you've had for a while to dial up a notch or two and hit *excruciating*.

The person you've planned to meet to attend the final talk with is running several minutes late, so you rush to be seated before the speaker begins.

Your feet hurt in the new shoes you bought for the dinner last night, the dinner where you drank too much, so your head is fuzzy, so you're in the queue for a coffee, and that's when you notice the person in front of you is the agent a friend introduced you to that morning.

"So what are you writing?" they ask.

"I've recently finished a novel," you reply.

"What's it about?" they ask.

Your head is full of highlights from the talk you've just attended. You haven't read your novel for a month or so. What do you say?

This happened to someone from my class at HWI.

Imagine you're in that situation. Start the timer. You've got four minutes, and that's being generous. Think of a work in progress or completed work that you'd love to find a good home for. If you have a novel, that's great. If you haven't got anything, make something up.

Jot down bullet points about what you'd tell the agent, or have the conversation in your head.

Four minutes up yet?
↓
No
↓
Keep going
↓
Four minutes up yet?
↓
Yes
↓
STOP

Did you get the gist of what your potential submission is about across?

No? That's too bad.

You've blown it.

The lesson here isn't that so-called elevator pitches don't always take place in elevators, but that you probably need a cogent description in your head for the work you're trying to find a home for.

Take novels for example. Remember the elusive one word story mentioned in "Story Structure" (chapter five)? If you summarise a novel into a few sentences, it can lose its individuality.

What can you say that will make your work stand out from the crowd?

How can you intrigue a potential agent or publisher?

You can find resources online to help you write a succinct yet engaging query letter. It's not easy. As we'll see when we discuss synopses in "Other Ingredients for a Book" (chapter twelve), the shortest things are often the most difficult.

# Chapter Ten

## Writers' Block and What's-the-Pointism

What's the point of polishing your writing to achieve publishable standard when no one wants to publish it?

The demons that haunt social media pop their filthy heads up and tell you you're useless, because everyone in InstaBluToX land has progressed at a faster rate than you have. What happened to you?

You are a failure.

What's the point of staying awake until silly'o'clock revising your competition entry for the hundred and eleventh time, to push *send* at a minute to midnight and immediately find a glaring plot hole you hadn't noticed, not even after one hundred and ten redrafts?

How can you call yourself a writer when everything that's coming from your metaphorical pen is lame?

You're only doing this as a hobby. Why are you spending days trying to squeeze out another chapter? You're avoiding seeing friends, not exercising enough, but you've got to get this done, though hardly anyone will read it. So why?

Is there any reason you couldn't stop writing and take up crochet instead?

You've tried a list of prompt words. You've placed creative constraints on your writing in order to stimulate it. You've taken yourself somewhere beautiful to write. There's a deadline looming, so why did you spend an hour watching videos about how ants communicate, and another on giant jiggle cakes? It's not as if ants or cake feature in your work in progress. Is it? So maybe watch one about making cake-filled moulded chocolate shapes instead?

Why did you send a critique partner a suggestion that you've since discovered is clearly wrong? How are they ever going to get any value from what you give them?

What's the point of writing stories about characters that you love who are not real, when there are real people dying in the world due to the stupidity of mankind and the indiscriminate violence of microorganisms?

What's the point of writing something funny when there's so much sadness in this harsh and desperate world?

What's the point of sitting staring at a blank screen erasing every sentence you write because it's shitty?

What's the point of wasting precious time making up pretend people when you ought to do something useful instead?

Why take yourself and your hobby so seriously when it's just a bit of fun? But are you having fun? If it's fun, why is it such hard work?

Why are you trying to get published when all that matters is that you're having fun? That's what your friends and family tell you, so why don't you listen to them and watch something on television like a normal person instead? There's no need to strive for anything better, is there?

What's the point of standing in front of a group of people and reading something you wrote? Why would they want to hear *you?*

What's the point of having a hobby where you spend more money than you could ever make from it? What's the hourly rate? Holy shit!

What's the point of even pretending you're trying to meet that deadline when you've indulged in every form of avoidance known to humankind?

There isn't really any point to most things.

We just exist.

Now we've got that out of the way, shall we carry on?

You deserve a little treat after reading all that. Here's the recipe for this chapter:

## Gulab Jamun

Indian sweets are often milk based. Traditionally, milk would be gently heated, stirring constantly until it reached the desired consistency. Yawn. It's easy to create shortcuts using modern ingredients such as ricotta cheese or powdered milk. The results aren't the same, but at least you're not standing over a hot stove for half a day. I wish there were similar short cuts available for writing, especially when you're having a day when you can't see the point.

With word processing, perhaps the "find and replace" function is the writer's ricotta cheese.

## Ingredients

- 2½ cups powdered milk
- ½ cup plain flour
- ½ tsp citric acid
- ½ tsp baking soda
- ½ tsp salt
- 2 tbsp melted butter or ghee
- approximately 150 mL milk
- 2 tbsp crushed pistachio nuts for decoration
- vegetable oil for deep-frying, plus some for rolling balls

## For the syrup

- 2 cups sugar
- 2 cups water
- 4 cardamom pods or ½ tsp powdered cardamom
- 4 strands saffron (optional)
- 1 tsp lemon or lime juice

## Method

- Prepare syrup by boiling sugar, water, cardamom and saffron if used, until a cooled drop feels slightly sticky. It shouldn't be allowed to reach the "stringy" stage. This will take approximately five minutes after the sugar has dissolved.

- Remove from heat and add lemon juice to help prevent the sugar crystallising. Cover syrup to keep warm, while you prepare the jamun.
- Mix powdered milk, flour, baking soda, citric acid and salt in a large bowl.
- Add the melted butter or ghee, and stir in sufficient milk to bind the mixture, forming a soft dough.
- Mix lightly. Do not knead.
- Heat oil in a pan or wok that can safely contain oil to a depth of 4cm.
- Coat the palms of your hands with oil so the mixture doesn't stick as you roll balls of approximately 2-3cm diameter.
- Test oil temperature by adding a small blob of dough. It should rise to the surface, but not brown immediately, as this would indicate the oil is too hot, and the jamun will over-brown before the inside cooks.
- Fry in batches until golden brown, and drain on kitchen towel.
- Check the syrup is still hot, otherwise re-heat until hand hot, not boiling. Remove from heat.
- Add jamun to the syrup, ensuring all the balls are covered in liquid.
- Allow to cool. After three to four hours, the syrup should have penetrated the balls.
- Garnish with crushed pistachio nuts and serve.

These sweets border on evil. They contain so much fat and sugar. But then, no one's going to live forever. Enjoy life a little.

Some cooks fry the jamun in ghee, but that would send me over my decadence limit.

Here's the exercise for this chapter:

# Rant

If you don't have any doubts or negativity about your writing, ever, you can leave this exercise out. Otherwise, time yourself for thirteen minutes (yes, thirteen), and spill out any reservations, anger, hesitation or murderous thoughts you've had about your writing.

After thirteen minutes, pick out some words from what you've written to make a positive sentence or two. (See the greyed out words in the body of the chapter.)

# Chapter Eleven

# The Writing Community

Writing is a lonely place.

You dig in the dirt for a perfect word, return to your piece the next day and replace that word with a better one. A week later the sentence containing the word is edited out. After a month you file the whole chapter in your recycling folder, and start another the next day.

Your main character is suffering, and you want to hug them, but you won't grant them that elusive happy ending, not because you are cruel, but because the story is so full, so intense, so profound; who knew pain could be so good?

Then you turn at a fork in the writing road, fall off the edge of the world and follow the character into their adventure.

While this is happening, you don't set foot outside your door, except to perform basic functions. You don't speak to anyone apart from the people you live or work with, and sometimes you don't hear what they say because they're not immersed in the world of your story.

I don't mean to create a vision of the lone writer immured in a stone vault, chained to a typewriter, skin wan from lack of sun, but it can feel that way when you're working to a deadline. You disappear into the warren of your mind to emerge later, smelling vaguely of the spoor of your characters, eyes scrunched against the light to discover the world has changed while you were away.

If you *do* feel like that, perhaps it's time to get a life. Setting goals and working hard is fine, but this writing lark is supposed to be fun.

Some of the fun may come when you interact with other writers. This may not suit everyone. Some are not too fond of other authors. However, for many, mixing with other creative beings can be a positive thing. These people appreciate you're keen to re-attach yourself to your laptop as soon as the party is over. They understand the self-imposed isolation required to complete the perilous journey towards a final chapter. These people will sit at your table and read or write in silence with you, because they enjoy that kind of companionship. They'll share food and drink, though it predominantly happens at book launches. They'll spit on the floor with you when someone writes *must of* when they mean *must have*, and it isn't done in irony. They cheer your successes, encourage you as you swim through the rough seas of submissions and commiserate when you're inundated with rejections.

I mentioned the importance of camaraderie in the prologue as a reason for enrolling in a writing course. There are multiple reasons for networking with other writers in real life or online. These people offer technical advice on anything from how to insert a page break to the best way to acquire an ISBN.

I discovered what a McGuffin was from a classmate. This term, which was often used by Alfred Hitchcock, refers to something that acquires great importance in motivating characters, but is of limited intrinsic value. People quote the Holy Grail in the legends of King Arthur as an example that predates the term itself.

I learned about the Rashomon effect from a local author. It's something I've looked out for and identified in stories and films ever since. This is where an event is observed and shown from the perspective of multiple individuals, each version contradicting the others. It takes its name from Akira Kurosawa's film released in Japan in 1950, where a murder is depicted from different characters' conflicting perspectives.

Members of the writing community are laden with resources. Get to know these people. Among them, you'll find writers who want mutual critique.

I learned the value of critical analysis at writing school. In "Getting Your Work Out There" (chapter nine), I stressed the importance of redrafting. Critique is a useful tool for developing your work. I've mentioned it in various contexts throughout this book. Let's look at the process in more detail.

It's important to find well-matched partners. Classmates on writing courses are ideal. Though you may have varying levels of experience, you share common goals, and may be exploring similar topics together.

Choose partners carefully. In "Respect, and a Question" (chapter seven), I mentioned it's usually unwise to ask for critique from family members. In "I Don't Go to Nursery – The Art of Active Reading" (chapter two), I said my critique partners have provided much of my "further education" in writing.

Seek writers who have a similar level of experience, as it makes reciprocation more valuable for both parties. Match yourself with someone who has a similar output and provides feedback with comparable turnaround times.

Here are some tips for providing critique:
- Do you have time to take this on? If someone asks you to critique their 120k-word novel by next week, offer to do one or two chapters (and remind them about industry standards for novel length).
- Is the work within your scope of experience? If someone asks me for critique on poetry, I warn them it's not my strong point. If they were to ask me to offer feedback on work set in a period of history I'm not familiar with, I'd suggest they ask someone else.
- Is their title engaging?
- Does the introductory sentence / paragraph / chapter meander without getting straight to the "meat" of the piece?
- Read the work more than once. I prefer to work on electronic copies, but others prefer hard prints or vocal feedback. I make tracked comments on the first read, add more on the second, checking the original ones, modifying them if the issues have been addressed further on in the text. I conclude with a concise summary that highlights structural elements that may need further work, or ideas about how the chapter relates to the arc of the whole if it is part of a longer piece.
- Focus on characterisation, story arc, pacing.
- Remain as objective as possible. Don't allow your personal grievances to enter the equation. I have a pet peeve regarding stories featuring kidney transplants. I'm not sure why I'm so emotional about this, except writers don't always research thoroughly and therefore write non-scientific crap that irritates my internal lab-nerd. I have to leave that stuff at the door when I enter the writer's world, because that shit's about me, not them.
- Point out where additional research may be of benefit.

- Your role isn't as a proofreader, however there's no harm in pointing out consistent grammatical errors if you notice them. It's helpful to identify continuity errors and conflicts. You don't have to solve them.
- Does the plot pass the plausibility check?
- Are the characters' motivations convincing?
- Can you suggest ways of enhancing the flow of the language, for example varying sentence length?
- Point out unnecessary repetition of words or concepts.
- How can the author add depth and nuance?
- Are any underlying meanings or themes coming across clearly? Conversely, are they too obvious and do they lack subtlety?
- Be honest. Don't limit your critique to praise alone if someone has requested feedback, otherwise what can they learn from the process?
- Modify your critique according to the level the writer is at. Be gentle towards newer writers. Remember those terrifying days of receiving critique early in your writing journey? Not had any yet? See tips below for receiving critique. "Commend, recommend, commend" works well for anyone, but sandwiching your most constructive comments between positive areas you have identified is helpful for starter writers.
- Always find *something* positive to say, even if it is only to point out your favourite parts, or bits you dislike least.
- Don't take over. It's their work.
- Have they concluded their story / poem / chapter in a satisfactory manner?
- Don't expect the recipient to follow your suggestions. I've seen the *bought* instead of *brought* error make it through to the printed version of a book despite my critique, which was somewhat perplexing. However, most of the time, the writer is simply

making a choice, and their choice isn't the same as yours. If you raise a question, it is in order to make the writer think about the point. They are not obliged to answer you.
• Be open to the fact that you may learn something from their writing.
• Don't worry about subconsciously plagiarising their work. You'd need a weirdly accurate memory to regurgitate their words verbatim without remembering you'd read it somewhere. If, however, you do recognise strong echoes in your own work, it might be wise to change them.
• Be respectful. There's no call for being rude. Thank people for sharing, especially if it's the first time you are offering that person critique.
• Encourage the writer. Be generous with your suggestions and time. If they feel like giving up, but you believe in their project, let them know.

Here are some tips on receiving critique.
• Ensure the work is ready prior to sending out. Polish it as much as you can, even if it's a first draft. You shouldn't rely on critique partners / beta readers to correct spelling or add apostrophes you plan to "put in later".
• Acknowledge receipt of the feedback you were sent, even if you can't bear to read the comments immediately. Someone has given their time. I've provided critique on request to people who have not responded to my email containing the feedback I gave them. I'm not looking for thanks, though that would be appreciated. But when they don't reply, I don't know if they are devastated by my comments or whether my correspondence is sitting in their spam folder while they wonder why I'm such a slack arse.

- Feedback can be crushing, especially early in your writing career. Remember the person is offering critique on your writing task, not criticising you. Brush yourself off, get back on the writing bike, and revise your work.
- Don't be defensive. If you disagree with a suggestion, simply don't act on it. This becomes obvious when receiving feedback from a group, as you may receive contradictory ideas. It's sensible not to seek critique from too many people, as conflicting suggestions can become unwieldy. Select people with whom the mutual process works well, authors whose writing you "get".
- I make notes about why I've ignored a suggestion if, for example, I plan to address the issue in a forthcoming chapter. I don't necessarily tell the critique giver. They'll know they've only made a suggestion, not a command.
- It's hard for people to respond only to the *crafting* of the writing without allowing personal taste to influence feedback. Bear in mind people may be sensitive about topics such as suicide, murder, adoption, religion, sexuality, abortion, politics or kidney transplants.
- Respect the person. Let them know, for example, if you change a setting or character's name partway through a novel, rather than waiting for them to work it out.
- Remember this is only part of the process. Ultimately, when your work is picked up, the publisher or editor will guide you on making the final changes.

In "Getting Your Work Out There" (chapter nine), I mentioned social media groups, for example in the flash fiction field. These have provided great sources of support as well as ideas for places to submit work.

Some online events offer group activities, such as writing a story or novel chapter every day for a month. They may supply prompts. I find the best aspect of these events is how writers encourage one another. I've rarely encountered negativity on these forums. Members of the group share their work and discussions take place, drawing on current affairs, etc, as we discover common themes influencing our work.

Some social media "friends" can become actual friends.

The writing "community" extends to professional bodies. Look at the services offered, such as mentorship and manuscript assessments, and consider joining. I touched upon these briefly in "Getting Your Work Out There" (chapter nine).

In "I Don't Go to Nursery – The Art of Active Reading" (chapter two), I talked about timetabling, i.e. breaking up your writing time into snippets in order to improve efficiency. It could be something as mundane as hanging out the washing, which can help in more ways than one. You can draw on all life experiences in your writing. My fabled picture book features a magical washday event. However, some activities enhance creativity. You may solve plot problems or find an elusive word while in the shower, on a walk or when you're drifting off to sleep.

Meditative activities can refresh your mind when you return to the keyboard. I'll elaborate on these in "Ancillary Activities" (chapter thirteen). But the reason I mention this here is because it's gratifying to share some activities with other writers. I'm thinking more of scheduling walks with them, or the activity suggested below, rather than have them come and do your laundry for you.

Writing is a lonely destination, but you need not always be alone there.

Here's the recipe for this chapter:

## Stone Painting

This is another activity, rather than something food-based. FFS, don't eat these. If you leave them where young children may find them, make sure they are large enough not to fit inside a small mouth.

I admitted to having kleptomaniac tendencies in "Sets & Drugs & Rock & Roll & Shady Characters" (chapter six). You'll discover why here.

## Ingredients

- stones with a smooth surface, from 1 to 15cm in diameter (see safety note above)
- acrylic ink pens of varying nib widths
- acrylic paints, household paint dregs or test pots (water washable, not gloss)
- paint brushes, cotton buds, dotting tools
- varnish, or artist's spray fixative

## Method

- Wash and dry the stones.
- Decide which side is the top.

- Add a plain background if desired. A broad (15mm) nib acrylic pen works well, as does a coat or two of acrylic or household paint.
- When dry, colour the reverse with the same or contrasting colour. I only do this if I've been messy. Otherwise I allow the stone's original features to show on the bottom.
- Create your design.
- Allow the paints or inks to dry.
- Varnish the stones, observing any safety guidelines particularly for sprays.

I work on several stones at the same time, so I can move from one to another as the ink or paint dries on the one I've recently worked on.

If you want to paint a representative image in a "painterly" style, use a brush with acrylic paints rather than pens, because blending will cross-contaminate your pen nibs. I rarely do this, as I prefer to create abstract patterns that are sympathetic to the shape of the stone.

Symmetrical patterns work well in terms of aesthetics and meditative potential. There are videos online on how to paint mandalas, which can be very effective. I start with a solid circle in the centre of the pattern (which may be off centre on the stone). Then I imagine a circle outside this and add dots in a different colour at 12 o'clock and 6 o'clock, followed by 3 o'clock and 9 o'clock. After that, I'll add one or more evenly spaced dots between each pair of the "clock face" dots.

Take a different colour and create another circle a little further from the centre by positioning a dot equidistant from each pair at the inner circle, creating an alternating pattern.

Add more circles until you approach the periphery of the stone. You may choose to extend the pattern further and have part of the outer circles "fall off the edge" if the stone is oval shaped. The outer circles can have larger spots.

Add final embellishments, such as a contrasting blob, a circle of tiny dots within or surrounding bigger spots. Use a pen with a narrow nib for this.

If you are stuck for ideas, search online for stone or rock painting. This is where you'll also find suppliers of acrylic ink pens and "dotting tools". These tools are pen-sized objects with a metal sphere at the end, available in a variety of sizes. The tip is dipped in paint and "dotted" onto a surface. If you make a series of consecutive dots, each will be smaller than the last, as the paint load diminishes. This can produce an attractive effect.

Some people use templates or paper circles as guides to create a more regular pattern. I prefer the organic feel of hand drawn images.


Finding stones can be complicated. When I began, I'd pick up the odd stone that had fallen away from public property. Over time I was drawn to pinch particularly smooth ones *from* the property. Although some of the properties concerned were building sites and car parks, it was still theft. But these people must have bought (brought?) their stones from somewhere. So I searched hardware stores, but the best I found were bags where fewer than 10% had smooth surfaces suitable for painting.

Earlier today, I visited a brackish lagoon known for its rough seas. It's a wild place. Huge rolling waves could kill you, and even if you took a chance in the water, a high level of toxic algae affects it, which could make you very sick. The place is also known for its smooth stones.

I may have accidentally picked up a few as I walked back to my car.

Placing stones requires some thought. Notwithstanding the danger posed by pretty coloured items being attractive to youngsters, convention dictates painted stones are placed in areas where others can find and enjoy them. It's considered unacceptable to leave them "in the wild", in places unmarked by human intervention. Brightly coloured stones covered in synthetic paints are unsympathetic to a natural environment. Outdoor areas that have been manipulated by people are fair game. My partner and I have placed stones in bike parks. Others leave them on urban bush walks. We've donated some to local charities who include them in care packages.

Here's the exercise for this chapter:

## Collaboration

Do you share a bond with another writer? Someone whose work speaks to you, a person who understands your writing? Have you ever written collaboratively with anyone?

Occasionally journals run editions or competitions featuring collaborations between two or more authors. I haven't seen many recently, which makes me wonder whether there are considerations about who holds the rights after publication. Even if you never submit the finished product, it's an interesting exercise to perform.

Decide what format you want to pursue. A short story or essay lends itself to this project. Compile a proposal including suggested word count, and how the structure will work. For example, will each person write alternating paragraphs or contribute a different character's point of view? How will the work be reviewed and assessed by each party as it progresses? How will the final piece be redrafted?

Offer the idea to writers who may be interested.

If you find a taker(s), see if they are happy with the structure you propose, or wish to modify it.

Set dates for when the collaborative work is passed from one author to the other. Decide between you when the thing reaches a natural conclusion.

# Chapter Twelve

## Other Ingredients for a Book

Yesterday, I read an article on how food waste contributes to greenhouse gas emissions. The authors challenged readers to cook something once a week using abandoned items that had been stored in a cupboard for some time.

The practice reminded me of the days when I lived in the basement flat in the north of England. Disregarding the fact that there were rarely any spare beans, lentils or flour left in any of our store cupboards, my friends and I would eat *anything*. It didn't matter if the components went well together or were nutritionally balanced or not. Food was food.

One friend learned to forage for edible weeds and fungi using an illustrated library book. We went fossicking for food once. He borrowed his mother's rubber gloves. The nettle soup turned out well, but the shaggy ink cap stew was mediocre.

Another friend introduced us to nasturtium leaf soup and pickled ash keys, a preserve made from the fruiting bodies of ash / Fraxinus trees. Nasturtium flower petals added a mustardy flavour to his salad.

There was a near miss a third friend had with a different sort of mushroom. At least they ended up in a police cell, not a hospital ward or mortuary.

Using ancient ingredients seems like an act of faith. Blind faith in our case, because some items in our pantry predate our moving to this house ten years ago. As the lentils, dried beans or speciality flours have long since been dispensed into secondary containers and lost any connection to their supposed expiry dates, it's hard to say for certain some of them don't pre-date our last house move by *another* ten years.

Should we eat them?

The sniff test is pretty reliable for many dry goods, but not failsafe.

Why are there so many items in life that can poison you? Shrubs pretending to be herbs, toxic algae, fiendish fungi and antediluvian lentils aside, isn't it a miracle that the human race survived and evolved over millennia at all? Don't even get me started on the vulnerability of human infants. How did cave dwellers manage without baby listening devices and sterilisers? And if they didn't co-sleep, a lion could have popped in and eaten their son or daughter for a snack. I can't imagine them using an adjacent vestibule in the cave system for their child's sleep training.

Still, if you can avoid things that will kill you (excluding lions), making a satisfying meal from scrappy leftovers is a useful skill. Unlike making a book, when you *must* have the correct ingredients, and quality is important.

A word on self-publishing: once frowned upon as much as co-sleeping with your newborn infant, this practice has become respectable. Similarly, hybrid funding models where the author invests in part of the publication costs, for example the print run, have been offered by established publishers. However, you need to look carefully at the organisation's history to ensure they are legitimate and not a vanity press before you embark on this option.

In the past, self-published work had a poor reputation, because they included books full of plot holes, typographical errors, poorly designed covers and an odd distribution of words on the page. Don't self-publish without performing all the necessary steps to create a book properly.

You don't want to be that person.


When the mainstream publishing industry fell on hard times, many competent and experienced writers published their own books, as they were no longer receiving offers. They did so with an awareness of the ingredients that are required to make a book other than the preliminary writing.

Typically these writers employed professionals to perform the functions a conventional publisher would provide.

This includes structural editing for novels in particular.

I won't talk in detail about every ingredient required for a book. However I will discuss structural editing, also known as substantive editing as I'd indicated in "Story Structure" (chapter five).

A structural edit considers the manuscript as a whole, identifying inconsistencies in style, repetition, whether timelines work properly as well as the story structure itself.

Some aspects of this are similar to a developmental edit, which is an overview that tells the writer whether the manuscript is achieving its aims.

The objective of both is to help guide the author with subsequent rewrites so the work is closer to publication standard.

There's copyediting, also known as sub-editing, where the text is checked to ensure it conforms to a consistent style. This includes spelling (American versus British), capitalisation and punctuation. The copyeditor suggests improvements to sentence construction, and identifies use of passive voice, i.e. the use of passive voice is identified.

A proofreader corrects any remaining errors.

There are endorsements to request, and acknowledgements to be made.

Moving away from the things the writer understands well, there's typesetting. If you want to know about widows, orphans, rivers and kerning, you can find information about these occult practices online.

And what the hell is a dinkus anyway?

Then there's the cover artwork, cover and spine design. I touched on design in "Story Structure" (chapter five) in the context of picture books. Design is important for covers too.

A publisher needs to be aware of copyright permissions for any quotes used. If you self publish, find out what's required.

If you aren't publishing yourself, you need to subject your work to the submissions process, which I have covered in "Getting Your Work Out There" (chapter nine). In that chapter, I've also referred to the process of sending queries to agents.

For novels you require a synopsis. This is what remains after you leave your work in a food desiccator for a very long time. You have a page or two that is enticing and provides the essence of what your story is about.

A synopsis should contain a plot summary, details about where and when the story happens, the genre of your book, readership it is aimed at and a word count. There are some conventions when writing these. Typically everything is written in the present tense in the third person.

The synopsis is similar to the blurb that graces the back cover, except you include spoilers.

It sounds easy, but is fiendishly difficult. The temptation is to include a little bit of everything, but you can't. As I mentioned earlier, sometimes the shortest things are the most difficult to execute.


How do you physically make the book? We've already seen there's more to creating a tome than cutting scrap paper, and putting it together with string and staples. You have to weigh up the cost of printing locally versus off shore or print-on-demand (POD) – a less risky option with a higher unit cost. You need to assess print quality when proofing copies come through.


And then there's distribution and marketing. Everything before this is wasted if no one ever reads the thing. I'll mention more about this in "Where to Next?" (chapter fourteen).

It goes beyond the scope of this book to outline how all these things are done, but it's important to know they *need* to be done.

Here's the recipe for this chapter:

# Mum's Moses Curry

My mother invented this recipe in the mid 1970s. Mummy Ghosh was an excellent cook. She was versatile, and could throw together something delicious from whatever ingredients she had at hand.

Our family watched a television series featuring the Biblical character Moses circa 1974. We looked forward to each episode on a Sunday evening.

As I was a child, I'm not aware of the reason we ate spiced potatoes with homemade chapattis or "rooti" for six consecutive Sundays, but my siblings and I loved it, and we have all made Moses curry ever since.

Like most of Mum's recipes, quantities are approximate and adjusted to taste.

## Ingredients

- 1 tsp (ish) each of the following spices:
  - whole cumin seeds (jeera)
  - ground cumin (jeera)
  - asafoetida (hing) – a pinch
  - whole coriander seeds (dhanya)
  - ground coriander (dhanya)
  - ground black pepper
  - mango powder (aamchoor) or substitute approximately 2 tbsp lemon juice

- 1 whole green chilli, de-seeded and finely sliced (or ½ tsp dried red chilli flakes if fresh green chillies are not available)
- oil / ghee / butter (approximately 2 tbsp)
- approximately 1 kg potato, cubed and par-boiled
- salt to taste

## Method

- Pre-heat oven to 180°C if using (see below ★).
- Heat oil / ghee / butter in a large pan.
- Add cumin and coriander seeds and pinch of asafoetida powder and cook on a low heat for a minute.
- Add cumin and coriander powders, plus black pepper and mango powder (but leave out the lemon juice at this stage, if using).
- Fry lightly for a minute or two.
- Add potatoes, chilli pieces and salt.
- Stir and fry the mixture, sprinkling a little water if potatoes stick to the pan.
- Cook for 30-45 minutes until potatoes soften and flavours meld.
- ★ Alternatively, after coating the potatoes with the oil and spices, transfer to a baking sheet and cook in the oven (180 degrees) for 30-45 minutes if you prefer a crispier finish.
- Stir in lemon juice before serving (if using).
- Serve with rice, chapattis or naan bread.

It's worth trying to source the asafoetida (hing) if you can, as that is what makes this recipe so special. This spice is derived from the latex of the *Ferula* plant's root. It has a pungent flavour that has earned it the colloquial name, *devil's dung*.

Here's the exercise for this chapter:

## Stubs

Near the start of "The (Almost) Infinite Freezer" (chapter one), I listed partly formed ideas from my "stubs" folder. The exercise in that chapter ("Recycled Sandwich") repurposed pieces of your work that needed redrafting. This time, we'll do something using your stubs if you have any. Stubs could come from a bedside notebook where you collect thoughts you have upon waking. They could be snippets of interesting conversations you have overheard and noted. They could be the ideas that jump into your head for a new novel when you're seven eighths of the way through your work in progress, and don't have time to develop a new concept.

Select ten phrases.

If you don't have anything, open a book or magazine at a random page and copy six to ten consecutive words starting at the seventeenth line of the writing.

Do this ten times.

## Ingredients

- ten phrases / collections of words acquired as detailed above
- imagination
- something to time twenty minutes with

## Method

- Set your timer for twenty minutes and write without stopping, incorporating at least seven out of the ten snippets you collected above.
- At the end of twenty minutes, review what you have written. Pare away any excess "fat". It doesn't matter if you lose some of your original phrases. They have served their purpose as prompts. Later, expand on what you have to create a piece of short fiction.

If you don't already have a folder containing potentially useful tidbits that might be useful ("stubs"), you may want to consider creating one.

# Chapter Thirteen

## Ancillary Activities

The day job.

Unless you are independently wealthy, very old or a criminal, it's likely you devote a considerable number of hours a week to something unrelated to writing.

Some authors earn sufficient amounts from putting words on paper to pay the bills, and can therefore write full time, but they are the minority. Many of us don't make enough from our writing most months to purchase a small sandwich.

Employment might drain your mind and exhaust you, but it shouldn't kill your literary output. Your day job might inform your writing. You can observe people in the workplace; steal their mannerisms, charm or physical appearances for your characters. Inter-personal battles and willy waving provide source material for conflict in stories.

Having to organise the hours in your day can improve efficiency. You allocate a chunk of time to professional activities and carve up the remainder between eating, sleeping, adult responsibilities and play. If playtime is precious, you tend not to waste it. You're less likely to procrastinate if you know you only have thirty-seven minutes before you have to stop writing chapter thirteen in order to wash the dishes, prepare a packed lunch, or paint a stone.

Have you noticed your efficiency increase when you know you have to leave for an appointment in ten minutes? You try to squeeze out another six sentences that would normally take an hour. You might use part of that hour vacillating and revising on the job. And the weird thing is that ten-minute sentences are occasionally better than their sixty-minute counterparts. It's an example of restriction increasing your freedom, or constraints helping you to focus, as I alluded to in "Story Structure" (chapter five).

I mentioned timetabling in "I Don't Go to Nursery – The Art of Active Reading" (chapter two). Allocating time to a variety of activities can help the creative process. You simulate the furious spate of activity that occurs ten minutes before you need to leave for an appointment, though you don't actually go anywhere. You simply take a break from what you're doing, and do something else. Then you go back to what you desperately want to do i.e. write the next chapter.

You can break your writing time up by dedicating ten minutes here and there towards work / study related activities, household chores or sex – it doesn't matter what you choose. And for those of you who are touchy about these things, I'm not being literal about the ten minutes here – only that it's a finite measured amount of time.

If you have dependents or are busy for other reasons, you don't have to put much thought into this. Your constraints will naturally channel your writing into limited periods.

However, if you have the luxury of spare time, it makes sense to actively divide your writing sessions. People can use minutes less efficiently when they have plenty.

An absorbing activity is ideal. When I mentioned precious playtime earlier, I used the example of stone painting, which I've described in "The Writing Community" (chapter eleven). It's a good one to dip in and out of, as it doesn't require much effort to set up or tidy away.

Other ideas include walking, meditation, playing sport, driving somewhere new, playing music, knitting, sewing, carpentry and gardening. Do whatever works for you.

Here is the recipe for this chapter:

## Creative Journalling

This sort of journal frees up the creative process, which can be useful when you hesitate to start writing on a clean page / word document. The journal in question can be a plain exercise book or notebook.

Alternatively, obtain an old hardback book someone's throwing out. Libraries sometimes have sales and you can pick up discontinued books cheaply. It doesn't matter what the book's about. If it has pictures they can add to the background texture and be incorporated into the work. I use an old interior design book from the 1980s.

## Ingredients

- a book
- paints, crayons or coloured pens
- glue
- scissors
- old magazines or newspapers
- found objects such as feathers, shells, tickets, whole spices, fabric
- needle and thread
- something to create atmosphere, such as music, candles, perfumes

## Method

- Give yourself permission to deface the book.
- You could paint the cover and add a title.
- Don't necessarily work from the beginning. Start in the middle or the end.
- Using a fat marker pen, write automatically for the duration of a piece of music. Use two pieces: one you know and love, another you've never heard before.
- If you're using an existing book, highlight selected words to create sentences that are unrelated to the original text.
- If using a hardback book, glue pages together to make robust surfaces for your work. Paint pages white, or stick sheets of plain or coloured paper over the original surface.
- Collage ripped coloured paper to make an abstract image to write on.
- For large books, remove some pages as the journal grows so it doesn't become too fat.

- Add things to the book, e.g. old photos, pictures from magazines. Include items with nostalgic value, such as cinema tickets.
- Write words triggered by the visual images you've created. They can be stories, poems or affirmations.
- If you don't want to handwrite directly over your collages and drawings, print or write the text on pieces of paper and stick them into the journal.
- Sew torn scraps of paper or fabric onto the pages.
- Draw something, for example a seashell, without looking at the page. It's a good way of freeing up your creativity. Your drawing won't look much like the original. Wind some words around the curves and lines you have made.

Can't draw? Who cares? This is not about technical competence. It's to liberate your creativity. This can be an enjoyable activity to do with someone else. Deface a page with a friend / partner.

Here's the exercise for this chapter:

## Character Building

A different way to create imaginary people, you may find this activity takes you to unexpected places.

## Ingredients

- your journal, if you have one, otherwise use scrap paper
- old magazines or newspaper
- glue
- scissors
- something to write with

## Method

- Cut or tear four images from a magazine, for example people's heads, machines, animals or a section of landscape.
- Stick them onto single or consecutive pages of your book, or one or more sheets of paper.
- Add to the images. For example, draw a stick figure body to a head. You could have human hands protrude from the side of a fish, feet on the bottom of a car, wheels beneath a face. Don't spend too much time on this. It's only an exercise to free up your mind and get ideas flowing.
- Now time yourself for twenty minutes and write a story about the character(s), creatures or scenes you've created. You can write directly on the pages, or separately, and attach to the journal / pages afterwards.

Finished?

Good. You can return to your work in progress.

Later, see if you can use all or part of the story based on the images in a new piece of work.

# Chapter Fourteen

## Where to Next?

My whole body is aching.

I've taken my own advice and have interspersed writing with other activities. I've decided to attend a Zumba class at the local sports centre.

Things get off to a bad start when a woman in vibrant pink leggings and matching trainers approaches me. We're waiting for the B.A.T. (bum / abs / thighs) group to vacate the hall.

"Are you here for Zumba?" she asks.

"Yes," I say, "and I'm scared it's going to be fucking hard."

"So, it's your first time?"

"Yes," I reply. In truth, I eventually remember I've tried one of these exercise dance classes a decade ago, but I haven't recalled why I promised myself I'd never return until it's too late and I'm being sucked into the room with others in bright coloured meshwork leggings.

"Oh, it's easy," the lady in pink says. She puts her water bottle on the dais at the front. "You'll love it."

"You've been before then?" I ask.

"I'm the instructor," she replies.

I'm the oldest person in the room, the only one who doesn't look as if they've been doing Zumba every day since the age of three. Beautifully toned legs and lithe bodies they have – every single one of them.

Everyone starts moving. There's music blasting from the sound system, and people step in unison. I try to copy my new friend, the instructor, but no matter what my brain tells my arms and legs, there's a two-second delay between seeing and doing, and I'm scooting off in the opposite direction to everyone else, almost colliding with numerous lithe bodies that move with alarming synchronicity and grace.

Then they start leaping.

I haven't leapt for years.

I try it.

Is my hip joint supposed to do that?

I glance at the clock.

We're three minutes into the routine – another forty-seven to go.

I'm never doing Zumba again.

But at least I timetabled something to break the writing up, so I'll be super efficient on the home strait of this book. Right?

Maybe not.

After the Zumba class, I went food shopping and then cooked a pot of seafood chowder. A Zoom meeting to discover more about publishing and marketing children's books followed that. It could be useful if I ever finish the picture book.

"Never submit a picture book complete with illustrations," they said.

"I know," I thought, and wondered for the forty-seventh time whether I should give up on the picture book.

Later I critiqued a short story, which involved background reading on the classification of male singing voices, inventive sexual positions and the introductory bars of a well-known piece of opera music.

The laundry needed doing. It was a great drying day. The cobwebs definitely had to be swept off the porch ceiling, but I probably didn't have to sing karaoke on YouTube for an hour.

Although I didn't resort to mirror glazing a cake, this behaviour smelled suspiciously like avoidance.

Humans are contrary creatures. Am I so thrilled at the prospect of finishing the final chapter of this book, that I'm sabotaging my own goal? Leaping about in a room full of athletic Zumbians (is that a word?) and giving myself delayed onset muscle soreness isn't my favourite way to spend a Saturday morning. The soreness wasn't delayed that much either. I had limped from the hall, trying to recall whether we had anti-inflammatory pills at home.

No more avoidance.


What do you do after your book comes out of the oven?

You've redrafted, responded to critique and checked for typographical errors. If required, you've written a synopsis. You've put the manuscript away and checked it again later.

It's ready to send out.

Skip forward to the point where you have an offer of publication. (Sorry if I make that sound easy, but you know about the hard yards from earlier chapters.)

What do you do now?

In "Other Ingredients for a Book" (chapter twelve), I touched on promotion, distribution and marketing. Everything you've done before this point may provide personal satisfaction but little else, if no one wants a copy. Books are meant to be read.

You can allow yourself a celebratory mirror-glazed cake or some of those Kryten-shaped chocolate thingies. But no waiting around to see whether the new baby attracts good reviews or is optioned for a movie. You have work to do. Those reviews don't happen by themselves.

By now, you're likely well into writing your next project, because there's little point waiting to see what happens with the last book before you start the next.

Now you need to break away from the new work to help your newly published book sail into the ocean.

Remember in "Getting Your Work Out There" (chapter nine), I mentioned how it was important to collaborate with your publisher to promote your book? I also noted the level of funding available affects what advertising potential there is.

If there's an agent involved, they may help with overseas publishing rights and appointing a translator.

A mainstream publisher will have links with booksellers. These are the people who move product onto bookshop shelves. They occasionally list books from independent publishers, but without promotion, the title may not get much further.

If you self-publish, or your book is with a smaller independent publisher, you won't have access to the services multinational companies provide. You need to be proactive. This includes organising a book launch. Some authors have more than one. They plan mini book tours in cities where they may have contacts.

Prepare your book launch(es) well. If you choose to invest financially (cake ingredients don't come for free), make sure you're doing something you'll enjoy anyway, rather than seeing your expenditure as something you expect to get a good return on. Think of it as a party, rather like organising your own birthday party. (There's more on that later.)

While your loyal friends might attend regardless, you can attract others by making the event entertaining. Plus you want those loyal family members and friends to have a memorable time, don't you?

Ideas for entertainment include inviting established writer friends to read or perform. You can provide high quality food and drink. Consider hiring live music, depending on the venue, and of course there must be cake.

Some bookshops support local writers. They may offer their premises for a launch. They might charge a small fee for refreshments, etc, but they often fund the staffing required to keep the premises open after hours. One drawback is that you need to invite every local person you know to get a decent turnout; otherwise it's unfair on the retailer. They're hoping for sales of your book, and as a bonus any other books people might buy given they'll have opportunities to browse.

If you're the sort of person who finds self-promotion excruciating, a bookshop launch may not be the best choice. However, if you go to the expense of hiring premises, you're going to need the numbers if you want to defray part of the cost. Also, you need a decent-sized audience to create a good atmosphere for people who *do* attend.

Make sure your books are available, and physically in your hands before the launch. I had a near miss with my first book, so now I don't plan the date until I'm certain I'll have copies in my possession.

Incidentally, that first book featured an image of a mirror-glazed cake made by artist Deb Williams on the cover. I ordered a cake topper featuring the cover to decorate a cake, because it appealed to my sense of the absurd: an image of an image of a cake to go on a cake.

An absence of books isn't the only reason these events may be cancelled. Foolishly, I planned to amalgamate the launch of my second book with my sixtieth birthday bash. I organised musicians, sing-alongs, catering, wait staff, and a fancy dress theme for which I ordered a costume that never turned up. We were going to have readings from other authors, an M.C., and of course every imaginable form of cake I had in my repertoire.

I stopped short of hiring jugglers, though I did ask a fire-eater if she'd do a performance on our deck.

The launch was cancelled due to COVID-19, which probably affected many writers, but at the time it felt as if I was the only one.

The launch of my third book was very conservative in comparison, but we still had fun (and lots of cake).

Make enquiries with local papers and magazines to see whether they can promote your book or the launch on their "forthcoming events" pages.

Approach bookshops that market books like yours to see if they'll hold copies on a sale or return basis.

Liaise with festival organisers, locally or further afield. I was lucky enough to be invited to run a workshop at a festival I attended overseas while on holiday a few years ago. I sent proposals through, telling them I was coming over from New Zealand for their event. They're always looking for variety.

Update your website.

Advertise your book on social media. You may choose to create pages dedicated specifically to the new title. Invite people to follow. Send personalised direct messages, but not to every contact, only those with whom you have genuine interactions. Otherwise, you'll develop a reputation for being a nuisance.

Contact local radio stations aiming for an interview about the book.

It won't kill you to send a synopsis or blurb to national radio or TV stations. It may be cringe-worthy, and you likely won't get a response, but you have to try these things if you want people to read your work.

Remember to submit to "new release" bulletins with any literary societies or social media groups you belong to. Enquire whether they organise functions where authors can give presentations.

You could create an entry on social cataloguing sites such as Goodreads, so readers can post comments.

Invite people who have given positive feedback to write a review and submit to journals or magazines that publish them.

Contact your alma mater. Writing schools may want graduates to present to students so the new writers can see what happens after the course.

Other ideas include organising writing workshops in the relevant genre, which include a complementary book. The entry fee covers the cost of hiring the venue and presenter, plus the book. Libraries may support these activities.

Be imaginative.

It's time consuming, but if you don't do anything, it's unlikely many people will read your book.

Here's the recipe for this chapter:

## Jayne's Mum's Cheesecake

I used to work with Jayne in the U.K. She brought her mother's cheesecake into work one day. We were seriously impressed when we tasted it. I wouldn't make this dessert often, as it's very rich. However, one sliver at a book launch won't kill anyone.

# Ingredients

- 2 x 250g packs of full fat cream cheese, brought to room temperature
- ⅔ cup caster sugar
- 250mL cream
- 250g full fat sour cream
- 2 large eggs, beaten
- 1 tsp real vanilla essence
- 1 packet digestive biscuits (20 biscuits)
- 150g butter
- topping of choice

# Method

- Pre-heat oven to 150°C.
- Grease an ovenproof dish (approx. 18cm square) with butter.
- Melt the butter (in a pan, or ½ - 1 minute in microwave oven).
- Crush biscuits in a food processor or place in a bag and use a rolling bin.

- Mix melted butter and crumbs in a bowl, and then press into the ovenproof dish to form the base.
- Cream the cheese and caster sugar together. Add beaten egg and vanilla essence. Stir in cream and sour cream, mixing well.
- Pour filling over base and bake for one hour.
- Check to see whether filling has solidified. It doesn't matter if it's a bit "floppy" while it's warm.
- If not ready, turn oven down to 140°C and bake for a further 5- to 15 minutes until solid.
- Chill for at least two hours.
- Serve topped with fruit such as fresh berries, slices of kiwifruit or bottled cherries.

I presume you haven't tried this recipe immediately upon seeing it. But if you did, I hope you survived the experience, so you can try the final exercise:

## Different Endings

This is an appropriate exercise for the end of the book.

Select a piece of writing that is complete, but not necessarily ready for submission. Or choose something that is sitting in your recycling folder ready to go out again. If you don't have anything that fits the category, select work that's already been published. If you find it too demoralising to toy with something that's reached the end of the road, use a piece written by someone else. It could be a novel you have just read, or a piece of short fiction found online or in an anthology. You could even select a film or television series.

Consider the ending. Is it satisfying? Does it draw elements together from the body of the work? Were there any unresolved issues? Is it best that they remain unexplained, or do they require closure? Were there any major "forks in the road" where the storyline could have gone a different way? Is it a happy ending? What if you made it into a sad one? Is it a sad ending? What would need to change earlier on to make a satisfactory happy end? If it was non-fiction, would its story value increase or decrease if the truth were replaced by a lie? Was the truth the *real* truth?

Now rewrite the ending in *five* different ways.

There's no time limit on this, as it will require some thought with a thorough understanding of the original.

Leave the five alternative endings to simmer while you do something else. (Have a slice of cake or paint a stone.)

Now review the five endings and compare them to the original. Is one of them better? If you're working with an unpublished piece, will you substitute the new ending?

If you do, check for any continuity errors you've introduced.

You don't want a last minute change to lead to a mistake.

Sometimes it is how we handle our past mistakes that teach us most in life.


Always learn from past errors.

I haven't.

I'm off to something they call "pump" at the sports centre soon, followed by "aquafit" on Monday.

It's been a blast writing this book.

I hope you have found something useful in it.

Now, where are those anti-inflammatories?

# Extra Exercises

As promised in "The Answer to the Question" (chapter eight), here are some more exercises, including several short ones. You can pop out the basic structure of a story even if you're busy, and redraft it when the opportunity arises. Others require more thought.

I've taken some from lessons I taught at the *Write On School for Young Writers* in Ōtautahi Christchurch. Others are new.

## Prompt Words One

Write for ten minutes, including the following prompt words: wizard, radish, time, organisation, template, bubble, reptile, drawer, shop, sock.

## News Article

Find an article from the news (current or historical). Focus on one character, and write a fictional piece from their perspective. (No time limit).

## Setting Exercise

Recall a room or building from your past – a place you lived or visited or a location seen in a film or on television. Do a rough sketch of a floor map of the place. Where are the doors / windows? Are there any emotions associated with this place? Jot down key words. Create a story in this setting where the main character overhears an argument they're not supposed to. Evoke senses besides visual (smell, sound, touch, taste). (Fifteen minutes)

## Voice and Vernacular Exercise

Write a piece for seventeen minutes in someone else's "voice". Consider whether the narrator comes from a different socio-economic background to you. What race are they? Do they speak with a different accent? Do they have a different morality from you? Include dialogue, in which you may choose to display the character's dialect.

## Prompt Words Two

Write for ten minutes, including the following prompt words: apathy, taste, plain, thorax, computer, tail, teapot, shaft, anagram, gas.

## Elaborate on a scene

Two cars are parked next to each other on the roadside beside a river. A man steps from one and lets two children out of the back. The children walk away from him towards a woman holding the door of the second car open for them. The narrator may be one of the characters or an observer, or you can use an omniscient perspective. (Eight minutes)

## Vandalism

Show your character's reaction after being told somewhere / something that is important to them has been vandalised / stolen / damaged and can't be accessed / used anymore.

You can use dialogue, but try to *show* how the person feels without describing their emotions directly.

If they do speak, focus on what their voice sounds like as well as their words. How do their stance and mannerisms reveal their feelings? How do other people respond to them? (Eight minutes)

## Disability Awareness

Write for ten minutes from the point of view of a wheelchair user / someone who is blind. The story takes place on Christmas morning, or a similar festival. If you aren't able bodied, write this from the perspective of someone with a different disability from yours.

## Hunger Game

Describe what it's like to be hungry to someone who has never felt hungry. (Five minutes)

## Emotional Responses

Select one or more of the following, and *show* the characters' emotions without spelling them out in a story that takes place at a train station. (Fifteen minutes)
- He felt tired.
- She loved him.
- They loathed one another.
- The children were bored.

## Prompt Words Three

Write for five minutes, including the following prompt words: tank, hospital, park, crescendo, map, tolerance, dynamo, water wheel, heart disease.

## Situation Drama

Write a three-minute response to one of these statements:
- Grandmother came home drunk.
- My mother is having an affair.
- My sister is leading a secret life. I'm the only one in the family who knows.

## Erasure

Tear a piece of text from a magazine or newspaper. Highlight chosen words to use in a story or poem. (Five minutes)

## Name Game

Write for twenty-five minutes. Take the first twenty seconds or so to rapidly write a list of names. They could belong to friends, family, famous people, politicians, etc, or you can invent them. Include middle / surnames / titles if you want.

    Choose two of the names, (A and B) and build them into characters. They don't need to resemble the individuals you took the names from. Write a piece where these characters argue or fight.

    Stop writing this part at ten minutes or earlier.

Now select two more names (C and D) from the list and write another piece / chapter that sheds further insight, or provides an alternative perspective to the characters A and B. For example, C might be the parent of B, and is talking to D about how B has had a disagreement with A.

Stop writing this part at twenty minutes or earlier.

Finally select two more names (E and F). Write a piece where the new characters shed light on what's happening to the people in the second story (C and D), and include a brief reference to the first characters (A and B).

## Sensory Maze

Write for ten minutes. Evoke the senses: sight, sound, touch, taste and smell as your main character finds themselves in a new situation. Perhaps they wake up in hospital, with little idea how they got there. Maybe it's the first day in a new school or job. Synaesthesia is a condition where stimulation of one sense leads to an automatic experience in a second sensory pathway. You may want to use this concept to enliven your writing.

## Prompt Words Four

Write for seven minutes, including the following prompt words: terror, paint, germ, appendix, lime, harbour, devil, train, sleeping-bag, porch.

## Time Trouble

Create a story that moves about in time. It could start or finish in the future. Include the present and / or past. Give some thought to the tenses you write in, to clearly indicate which time line you are in. Use signposts if necessary: gadgetry, the age of the character(s), etc. (Fifteen minutes)

## Automation

Write for two minutes without pausing using a stream of consciousness process where what you've written triggers the next part, which may or may not have an identifiable association. It doesn't have to make sense.

## Rhyme Time

Write for ten minutes. Take the first minute or so to source a list of ten rhyming words. They don't need to have the same number of syllables. You can find them online, in a rhyming dictionary, or pluck them out of thin air if you're good at that sort of thing. Now use the words in a piece that is *not* a rhyming ditty. Write about an approaching storm. Use rhyming words to help create a pattern that enhances the rhythm and flow of the piece. This is not easy to do, especially as you have the constraint of whatever words you cooked up at the beginning. Badly placed rhymes can make the writing sound annoying rather than enhancing it, but used well they can enhance the musicality of the piece.

## Memory

This exercise takes six minutes. Take the first minute to identify one of your earliest memories. Close your eyes and immerse yourself in that zone. Conjure smells, the feel of the air on your skin, and your emotions. Were you happy? Were you anxious? Try to gauge whether it is a genuine memory, a memory of a memory, or an assumption triggered by a photograph from your past. Let *you* from that time take control of the keyboard or pen, and write about that scene.

## Overheard Words

If you have a notebook or folder where you collect snippets of overheard conversation, select a sentence or two from there. If not, "snatch" some words from the radio / television / picked at random from a book. Write a piece set in a cafeteria, using the overheard / borrowed words. (Five minutes)

## Prompt Words Five

Write for seven minutes, including the following prompt words: skin, deer, odour, daughter, history, dandelion, action, idea, portent, slime.

## Angry You

Write for twenty minutes remembering a time or situation when you were really angry. Focus on what triggered the feeling and your responses. Transfer the anger to your character, but place them in a different situation. Let them have a proper moan about whatever is boiling their piss.

## Grief

Write for eleven minutes, plus you need some listening time. Play a piece of music that evokes a feeling of grief. It might be something that was used at a funeral, a song that reminds you of someone who is no longer in your life, or simply a sad piece of music. While you are still moved by what you listened to, write a story involving grief, drawing on experience or a historical event.

## Prompt Words Six

Write for fourteen minutes, including the following prompt words: tendril, past, paper, leg, egg, development, garden, larva, taste, temperature.

## Allegorical Insect Exercise

This piece will appear to be about an insect / insects, when its underlying meaning is something different. You could draw on current affairs or offer social commentary. (Ten minutes)

## Thing

Take five minutes to write a piece from the perspective of an inanimate object. Have it reflect on recent events.

## Times Ahead

Write for ten minutes, starting by quickly listing five to seven words relating to the future, without giving it much thought. Write a story triggered by the words.

## Strangers

Write for ten minutes about two characters who don't know each other, showing how they interact, for example at a party, job interview or on social media.

## Polyglot

Write for ten minutes incorporating words from another language. If you don't know any, look them up or invent them. The meaning needs to be hinted at from the context of the story.

## Surreal Past

This exercise is ten minutes long. Recall an event / experience from your early childhood. Write an account of the event / experience, but introduce at least three elements of surrealism into the story. For example, if writing about a scary music teacher, you could include something about the sleeping dragon that lives in the guts of the piano. If writing about a memorable holiday, you could add a part where the narrator (you) flies over a beach once the adults are asleep. Think of something impossible that is compatible with the scene.

## These are a Few of My Favourite Things

This exercise takes five minutes. Take one minute to list six to eight important things from your life. They could be friends, activities or attributes you admire. You can select television programmes, favourite foods or whatever comes to mind. Then write a short piece using at least four of the items. The story doesn't need to feature you, though it can if you want.

## Prompt Words Seven

Write for four minutes, including the following prompt words: heavy, tent, last, tight, order, chaos, thimble, danger, outside, hammer.

## Factual

Take five minutes to write a story about a significant meeting from your past. It could be when you met a new sibling, partner or colleague you like or dislike. For the first draft, report everything realistically. Focus on the setting, your emotions and include some dialogue.

## Distortion

Take ten minutes to change parts of what you wrote in the previous exercise to create hybrid fiction / memoir piece. You could redraft the original text, or use the ideas from it to create a new piece. Introduce a source of conflict if there wasn't one before, or eliminate one that was present. Consider changing the point of view. Twist the facts to make the story more interesting. Omit some of the detail you had in your earlier draft. Introduce additional (imaginary) characters if you like.

## Blah Blah Blah

Take ten minutes to write a piece that is almost entirely in dialogue. Suggested settings: a shop, under someone's bed, in a cinema or a factory.

## My Favourite Aunt

Write for fifteen minutes about a real or imagined aunt, from a child's perspective. Include a journey, revelation or secret and a piece of rope.

## Precious Object

Write for ten minutes, inspired by an object you own or have wanted to own. This can be poetry or prose.

## Prompt Words Eight

Write for nine minutes, including the following prompt words in a story that combines reality and imagination: sun, levitate, top, nightmare, understanding, typewriter, cloak, leg, water, horses.

## List

Write for five minutes in the form of a list, which features members of your family. Make some of the characters or features up.
Follow this format:
- Uncle Bernie is my father's brother. He smokes cigars and tells tall stories.
- Marama is my sister. She buys me the coolest presents, but steals them later.
- Lee is my stepdaughter. I take her clothes shopping, but she has terrible dress sense.

## Musicality in Your Hometown

Set this piece in your hometown (current or past), paying attention to rhythm and sound patterns e.g. assonance, rhyme, alliteration, etc. Vary the sentence lengths. (Fifteen minutes)

## Prompt Words Nine

Write for five minutes, including the following prompt words: driver, catchment, bead, drop, telephone, angry, definition, place, powder, hand.

## Historical Piece

Write for fifteen minutes, setting the piece in an era before your birth. Focus on authenticity, and how the style or "voice" is shaped by the time you choose.

## Future Food Fun

This story features food. At least half of it should be written using the future tense. (Five minutes)

## Diary Part One

Take two minutes to write an account about an event that happened earlier this week. (Five minutes)

## Diary Part Two

Rewrite the account from someone else's point of view. (Four minutes).

## Diary Part Three

Rewrite the events in parts one and two, but this time, they are observed by an "unreliable narrator". Have them introduce subtle lies as they talk about what happened. (Six minutes)

## Prompt Words Ten

Write for seven minutes, including the following prompt words: swimmer, couch, tennis, hotplate, armpit, uncle, brain, outside, monument, hamper.

## Animal Magic

Write for three minutes. Make a story set in your home from the perspective of a non-human animal, large or small. Someone has just died as the story begins.

## Random Generator

Tired of picking the same old names for your characters or settings? If you want to create something unusual, type five to ten random letters or symbols and let spell-check suggest a correction. If it can't, remove one or two letters until the algorithm finds something. Use the words as characters, place names or prompts in a piece of writing. No time limit for this one. Here is an example:

| Random letters: | Some removed: | Suggested correction: |
| --- | --- | --- |
| sm;fla | smfl | smell |
| dfoaifhj | doaifh | dovish |
| sngjhsrfs | sghsrs | shares |
| fjnufiyag | fnufiag | funfair |
| hgkhelw | hghew | higher |
| uighirhn | uighirn | bighorn |
| fjkef | fjkef | fake |

*Bighorn* offers his meat to the *dovish* girls at the *funfair*. Other butchers hold *shares* in the abattoir and demand *higher* prices. Those girls complain about the *smell*, and accuse Bighorn of selling *fake* venison.

I can see these characters: Bighorn, the well meaning but stupid oaf; the meek, yet cheeky dovish girls; the competitive meat market and the stink. But I would never have thought to create a scene like this without the prompts.

## Lost and Found

Have you ever lost something and found it years afterwards? Imagine this happens under the most unlikely circumstances. For example: "Tonight I found a pair of glasses I'd lost on holiday overseas three years ago. They turned up in the bathroom of a restaurant I visited for the first time." (Five minutes)

## Tall Tale

Write for four minutes. This piece should be rich in exaggeration, hubris and extreme ideas. Use dialogue.

## Current Affairs

Create a fictional piece based on recent current events: place a fictional character in a war-affected region, or an imaginary athlete or spectator in a real sporting event. If you can't think of a real situation, make one up, but write it in the *style* of a current affairs piece, such as a newspaper / TV programme. (Five minutes)

## Goodbye

Create a story or poem featuring a farewell or parting. (Five minutes)

# List of Recipes

| | |
|---|---|
| Prologue | Chocolate Almond Cake (p. 2) |
| Chapter One | Cake-filled Moulded Chocolate Shapes (p. 14) |
| Chapter Two | Gluten-free Moist Apple Cake (p. 25) |
| Chapter Three | Mirror Glazing (p. 36) |
| Chapter Four | Larcomas (p. 43) |
| Chapter Four | Blöd's Burgers (p. 45) |
| Chapter Four | Fruit Crumble Jumble (p. 46) |
| Chapter Five | How to Thread a Quilt Cover onto a Duvet (p. 58) |
| Chapter Six | Flat Bread with Chia Seeds and Rosemary (p. 72) |
| Chapter Seven | Making a Book – Literally (p. 84) |
| Chapter Eight | Nothing (p. 87) |
| Chapter Nine | Moroccan Lamb Tagine (p. 95) |
| Chapter Ten | Gulab Jamun (p. 103) |
| Chapter Eleven | Stone Painting (p. 115) |
| Chapter Twelve | Mum's Moses Curry (p. 125) |
| Chapter Thirteen | Creative Journaling (p. 131) |
| Chapter Fourteen | Jayne's Mum's Cheesecake (p. 142) |

# List of Exercises

| | |
|---|---|
| Prologue | Ten Minutes When You Must Write (p. 4) |
| Chapter One | Recycled Sandwich (p. 17) |
| Chapter Two | Emulation (p. 27) |
| Chapter Three | The Time Traveller's Mirror (p. 38) |
| Chapter Four | Crossing the Genre Boundaries (p. 48) |
| Chapter Five | Messing About with Time (p. 60) |
| Chapter Six | Who am I? Where am I? When am I? (p. 74) |
| Chapter Seven | Dirty Writing (p. 86) |
| Chapter Eight | Zilch (p. 88) |
| Chapter Nine | Elevator Pitch (p. 98) |
| Chapter Ten | Rant (p. 106) |
| Chapter Eleven | Collaboration (p. 118) |
| Chapter Twelve | Stubs (p. 127) |
| Chapter Thirteen | Character Building (p. 133) |
| Chapter Fourteen | Different Endings (p. 143) |
| Extra Exercises | Lots! (p. 145) |

# Author Acknowledgements

My teachers and mentors at the Hagley Writers' Institute, Ōtautahi Christchurch, who introduced me to the alchemy of writing.

Eileen Merriman, who helped me sift through my writing and take out the lumps.

Matt Potter, for providing the raising agent for several of the books I have baked to date.

Members of the writing community with whom I have shared the process right through to the cake on the table.

# About the Author

Originally from the U.K., Nod Ghosh lives in Ōtautahi Christchurch in Aotearoa New Zealand.

Nod graduated from the Hagley Writers' Institute in 2014.

Nod's published books include the novellae-in-flash *The Crazed Wind*, Truth Serum Press (2018); *Filthy Sucre*, Truth Serum Press (2020); *Toy Train*, Truth Serum Press (2021); *Love, Lemons and Illicit Sex*, Truth Serum Press (2023); *Throw A Seven*, Reflex Press (2023); and the novella *The Two-Tailed Snake*, Fairlight Books (2023).

Her short fiction has been widely published in New Zealand and internationally.

Nod has been a relief teacher at the Write On School for Young Writers Christchurch since 2017, and has conducted workshops including one that featured cake at the Bath Flash Fiction Festival in the U.K. in 2019.

Other roles include:
• Associate Editor *Flash Frontier, an Adventure in Short Fiction,* 2016-7.
• Judge for the South Island Writers' Association (S.I.W.A.) short story competitions 2016 and 2020, poetry competition 2017 and flash fiction competition 2022.

• Judge for the Takahē magazine short story competition 2019.
• Member of editorial team Flash Flood (UK NFFD), June 2020.
• Judge for the Bath Flash Fiction Award, October 2020.
• Guest Editor UK National Flash Fiction Day anthology 2021.
• Reader in Residence for SmokeLong Quarterly December 2020 to March 2021.
• Judge for the University of Chester Flash Fiction Youth Competition, March 2021.
• Facilitated workshop on flash fiction for the New Zealand Society of Authors Canterbury Children's Literary Hub, July 2023.

Nod has provided critique for many writers including Eileen Merriman, who has several young adult and literary novels published by Penguin Random House.

Further details can be found at: http://www.nodghosh.com/

# Also by Nod GHOSH
## from Truth Serum Press

truthserumpress.net/catalogue/fiction/

*The Crazed Wind*
978-1-925536-58-4 (paperback) / 978-1-925536-59-1 (eBook)
*Filthy Sucre*
978-1-925536-92-8 (paperback) / 978-1-925536-93-5 (eBook)

*Toy Train*
978-1-922427-49-6 (paperback) / 978-1-922427-56-4 (ePub)
*Love, Lemons and Illicit Sex*
978-1-923000-06-3 (paperback) / 978-1-923000-09-4 (ePub)

# Also from EVERYTIME PRESS

everytimepress.com/everytime-press-catalogue

## Resource & How-To Books

*School Daze* by Irene Buckler
978-1-922427-16-8 (available in paperback only)

*It's About the Dog* by Guilie Castillo Oriard
978-1-925536-19-5 (paperback) / 978-1-925536-20-1 (eBook)

*all you need is ... a whiteboard, a marker and this book!*
by Matt Potter (available in paperback only)
978-1-925101-82-9 (Book 1) / 978-1-925101-96-6 (Book 2)

www.ingramcontent.com/pod-product-compliance
Lightning Source LLC
Chambersburg PA
CBHW031259110426
42743CB00041B/746